FOUR YEARS'
SERVICE IN INDIA.

BY A PRIVATE SOLDIER

(Corporal John Ryder, formerly of the 32nd Foot,
and now of the Leicestershire Constabulary.)

The Naval & Military Press Ltd

published in association with

FIREPOWER
The Royal Artillery Museum
Woolwich

Published by
The Naval & Military Press Ltd
Unit 10 Ridgewood Industrial Park,
Uckfield, East Sussex,
TN22 5QE England
Tel: +44 (0) 1825 749494
Fax: +44 (0) 1825 765701
www.naval-military-press.com

in association with

FIREPOWER
The Royal Artillery Museum, Woolwich
www.firepower.org.uk

The Naval & Military
Press

MILITARY HISTORY AT YOUR
FINGERTIPS

...a unique and expanding series of reference works

Working in collaboration with the foremost
regiments and institutions, as well as acknowledged
experts in their field, N&MP have assembled a
formidable array of titles including technologically
advanced CD-ROMs and facsimile reprints of
impossible-to-find rarities.

*In reprinting in facsimile from the original, any imperfections are inevitably
reproduced and the quality may fall short of modern type and cartographic standards.*

THE EDITOR TO THE READER.

THIS work may be said to speak for itself. Its title is almost a sufficient indication of its purport and contents. Yet the mention of a few circumstances connected with its appearance before the public may not be superfluous.

The author is now a member of the Leicestershire Constabulary Force, into which he was admitted, with excellent testimonials as to his character before he entered the army and during military service. While in his present capacity, he laid before the Chief Constable, Mr. Goodyer, certain manuscripts, containing memoranda of his daily experience as a soldier, and these were found so interesting by that gentleman, that he lent the manuscripts to various acquaintances and friends, who all agreed in pronouncing the account they contained as well deserving general perusal. Mr. Goodyer then placed them in my hands, with a view to their examination, to determining whether the contents would be found worthy of publication. The result of this examination was, that the manuscripts were next entrusted to me to be printed; and I undertook the task of revising them, and bringing the work to completion. In the interim, the County Constabulary exerted themselves among their friends to raise a subscription-list. Their labours have terminated in a way which proves alike their creditable zeal to befriend a comrade, and the influence which a knowledge of their utility and worth have earned for them in their respective districts—in one or two months they obtained orders for thirteen hundred copies of the book!

The author having learnt to read and write after he became a soldier, his composition was necessarily very incorrect in expression, and in many respects ungrammatical; but though incorrect and ungrammatical, the bright ore gleamed through the rough vein of earth in which it was encrusted. And, though the language will be found at times rugged and plain, even to excess, it is the same kind of language that has found its way to all hearts, in the winning narrative of Defoe, and the world-known allegory of Bunyan—it is the speech of rural England, which even yet stubbornly refuses to mingle with the Norman and classic elements that frequently strive to blend with it—it is the almost uncontaminated speech of our Saxon and Scandinavian forefathers, in the presence of which every foreign word is, even at this day, recognized at once as an intruder.

Having advised the publication of the work, I naturally feel a share of responsibility in its introduction to the world. I know full well that its contents may be distasteful in some quarters, and that they will be open to misconstruction in others. The honest truth of corporal Ryder's narrative leaves it, I think, too palpable, that the private soldier's condition in India is not what it ought to be. The fearful number of deaths and prevalence of disease in the barracks; the very injudicious choice of their situation in some cases; the irregularity in the supply of rations; the too frequent exhibition of drunkenness, not only in the ranks, but among the officers; and other matters, too clearly attest the existence of neglect and abuse in the Indian army.

At the same time, it must be observed, that the good feeling subsisting between officers and men in that army,—and the way in which they share privation in the campaign, and danger in the conflict—are truly gratifying. The fearful loss of life in our own ranks, and the terrific slaughter of our enemies, on the open battle-field, with the horrid barbarities and unmanly outrages consequent on a siege, when read of by the quiet firesides and happy hearths to which this little volume will penetrate, will kindle sentiments of horror and disgust, and wonder at their reality. And there will be many who will say, " Away with war! Away, for ever, with a system that demands the expenditure of so much blood and so much treasure!"

This exclamation springs from a benevolent and honourable sentiment. Every one must, more or less, feel with it some sympathy. It contains the instinct which, we would fain hope, at some time or other, lingers in every human heart—the yearning after a utopia: a yearning never gratified.

Unfortunately, however, for these day-dreams, when we contemplate the present state of the world, the hard realities of life disperse them rapidly. It seems that at the very best, sometimes, our choice lies between two evils—not between an evil and a good; and this is not unfrequently an inevitable emergency in the inscrutable economies of Providence. Hence, the employment of warlike agencies by a great nation like this, in the maintenance and defence of British supremacy at home and abroad, is the alternative evil offered for our choice. Undoubtedly, if it were possible now to see Europe in the tenure of free and pacific peoples, and to hold British

India by means of moral force, it would be most desirable to do so; but it is not possible; and therefore we are bound, as a nation, to be prepared to preserve inviolate the liberties and privileges now exclusively enjoyed by the British race in Europe, and to maintain the sway of civilization in India—lest in Europe and Asia the lamp of freedom and progress be extinguished, and a moral and political darkness once more overspread them, involving them in the night whence they have for only a few centuries emerged. And above the thunder of cannon and the roar of musketry, and the shrieks of the dying on the plains of India—most melancholy and painful in all truth—I hear the clarion-blast of triumph for civilization, and progress, and Christianity, over the caste-bound systems of Asia, over its petty and sanguinary tyrannies, and over its hoary and blood-stained idolatries. Nor is the least inspiring element of satisfaction, to be derived from a contemplation of the late battles in India, the consciousness that British Manhood, while it has won the great prizes of empire in conflicts it has not sought, and has held them, not on the whole unworthily, it is still undegenerate—faces and conquers alike the fierce Sikh and the brave Affghan—and has given a pledge, that if the ark of liberty, now in its sole and peculiar custody, should be endangered by the hostility of European despots, the hands and the hearts of our fellow-countrymen are strong and stout enough to keep it inviolate from the assaults of all the hosts of an enslaved, a semi-barbarian, and a degraded Christendom.

JAMES THOMPSON.

Leicester, April 1853.

CHAPTER I.

ENLISTMENT—SERVICE IN IRELAND—THE VOYAGE TO INDIA.

I AM a native of Twyford, in the county of Leicester, and from childhood have had a strong inclination for the army; although my father (who is an old soldier, and was at Waterloo) always tried to set me against it, by telling me that for the least offence the cat-o'-nine-tails would be made use of. He would also describe to me the horrors of the battle of Waterloo, thinking in that way to turn my mind from a soldier's life; but instead of turning me, this only made me the more anxious to become a soldier; and I never was so happy as when I was listening to him talking about it; till at last he would say, " Boy, don't ask me any more foolish questions, for you will not understand me if I talk for a month, until you have been to see." He had served ten years in the 1st. Dragoon Guards; also, his brother and cousin. They were at the battle of Waterloo, and were all wounded. My father received three wounds, and his brother eleven.

Time passed on, and in the year 1843 I was in service at Nottingham. I had a good place, and a good master: he was a remarkably clean man, and we agreed very well; but at the same time, I had been watching the soldiers as they went to church from the barracks, and I thought it was the finest sight that I had ever seen. Their very looks made me wish I was among them. I wondered how they did to step so regularly, and was so foolish as to think their legs were all tied together. It was altogether a mystery to me, for I had never before seen soldiers, with the exception of one on furlough.

After seeing all this I was not likely to content myself long; so one night I went up to the barracks, and tried to enlist; but I was not high enough for them, as they were heavy dragoons—the 6th Enniskillens.

At the beginning of 1844, I made myself known to sergeant Dyer, of the 32nd. regt., who was then recruiting at Nottingham. He was a fine-looking man, and dressed very smartly. He was trimmed all over with silver lace, and wore an officer's cap; he did not lose an inch of his height, for he was very proud. One night he took me to his house (for he was a married man) to measure me, as I would not go to a public-house with him. The sergeant measured me, and said, "Barely 5 ft. 6 in., my lad; but you're young, and I shall try and get you passed." I had not quite made up my mind, so I did not enlist that night; but in a few nights after I was going down the Long Row on some business for my master, when I met the sergeant, and I said to him, "Well, I want a place." "That's right, my lad; thrust your body into the army, and make a man of yourself," said the sergeant. At the same time he held out a shilling, but I told him I should not take it there; so we went to his house, and I thus enlisted in the 32nd. regiment, being then in my twentieth year. I went straight away home, and told no one; although I saw my uncle and my sister: but the next day I told my uncle, and he told my master. They were both very sorry, and tried to persuade me to pay the "smart," and not go; but I would not consent. My master asked me if I had anything against his place; or what induced me to go? I told him that I had nothing against him, but I had made up my mind to enlist. The next day I told my sister, and she was almost ready to go beside herself.

On an afternoon a few days later, my sister's husband and I started from Nottingham to Twyford, a distance of about thirty miles; though I had agreed that he should not tell my father or mother that I had enlisted. We got as far as Melton that night, but it snowed so fast that we did not go any further. The next morning we arrived at home.

My father was surprised to see us there so early; but I said we had just come to see them, and that we must go back that night. My mother (poor old creature!) thought that all was not right, or I should not be going back so soon. Our secret was very near being found out, for my coat was hanging up, and my mother went to it, and was feeling in the pockets, and had got my duplicate in her hand before I saw her. I snatched hold of it before she had got it open, and told her that paper was not for her or any one to look at, and that she must not see it; so I got it away again. My mother was very uneasy all day. At four o'clock we started back. My father came about two miles on the road, and I told him that I had enlisted. The old man made a great trouble of it, and I felt very sorry for him; but before he left us, he bade me be a good soldier, and never desert my colours. He then bid me "good bye," and we arrived at Nottingham, by train from Syston, that night.

Early in the morning, shortly after, the sergeant came to say that I must be up at his house in an hour's time, for we were to march that morning at ten o'clock ; and I was glad that the order had come. At nine o'clock, the whole of the recruits had met at the Bull's Head: and when I saw them altogether a pretty sight there was! I was ashamed of being among them; for they were a dirty, ragged lot of blackguards—some of them then nearly drunk.

We started in charge of a corps of the Rifles ; for we were not all for one regiment. We were marching for Manchester, where my regiment was then stationed. On arriving there, we went to Tibb-street, where six companies were lying. The first soldier I saw belonging to the regiment was a man as sentry on the outside of the barracks. It was raining a little, so the sentinel was cloaked, and I thought I never saw such an object in my life before. He had on his knapsack, and shouldered his long musket with his bayonet fixed. I was now sick of my job, and I began to repent my bargain.

We did not stop here; we went to Salford barracks, where our head quarters were. On the way we met another soldier of the 32nd. I never saw such a poor-looking thing in my life. he was a thick, short man, and hump-backed. His dress was too large for him, and looked dirty. I had now seen quite enough of the foot-soldiers, and began to think I should not be a soldier long; but on meeting some more of the men, I saw they were smart and clean-looking, which put me in better spirits, and I afterwards learned that the other man we met was a pioneer.

On arriving at the barracks we went before the colonel, who was a keen, sharp man. He soon took a survey of us : he asked me many questions. He told me to take care of myself, and I should soon make a soldier. We then went to the hospital, and passed the doctor. We were ordered to remain in there until we had got our regimentals. We had been there about an hour, when a corporal came to take us to the tailor's shop to be measured for our clothes. I could not help looking at this corporal, for he stood 6 ft. 7 in. in height. After being measured we were brought back to the hospital, and now we were to commence soldiering.

The first thing that happened was—in came a man and said, " Where are those ' cruiteys ? ' " and then commenced and cut our hair off so short that I could not get hold of it. This hurt me more than anything. I could not help weeping to see my hair cut off as bare as though it had been shaved.

We were kept in the hospital two days. The second day we fitted on our clothes, which they had not taken much pains with; and on my remarking that mine were a deal too large, I was told that they were just right for my drill. We were then taken to the barracks, to the company to which we belonged— No. 4. company, then on detachment at Tibb-street. I was attached to the Grenadiers. On going to the barrack rooms, we passed some officers, when I heard one of them say, " He has got a watch now, but he will not have it long." I thought, " you will be wrong." It appeared he knew the tricks the old soldiers would play to get it out of me.

That afternoon we commenced drill for the first time, which we got on pretty well with. Many were the schemes laid to get me off, to spend my money and pawn my watch ; but I resisted them all. I was not liked among that sort of men because I would not join in with them. Being in the colour-sergeant's room, he had marked me, and saw that I resisted all. He took me under his own care, and very kind he was. He took my clothes which I had come up in, and put them away ; and if I did not wish to sell them, he said, I might send them home. So as I could not get one half their value, I sent them home to my brothers.

I found our rations very scant. I could have done with as much more very well; but in a short time I could do very comfortably with them, and with what little I could buy, and I was never without a pound in my pocket. I soon got on with my drill, and had my clothes altered to fit me. I now began to be altogether very content, and even proud when I walked out. I bought an extra kitt, so as to always have one clean and neat to show at kitt inspection.

One day, while standing on parade, the colonel was inspecting all the recruits; he was finding great fault as he came along the ranks, but when he came to me he took my cap off my head, and said he wanted to see them all like *that*, and that all should take a pattern by me for all my things. Another day at kitt inspection, some time after, the officer was finding fault with some of the kitts; but when he came to mine, he told them he wanted to see them all like it. One old soldier, who felt rather nettled about it, spoke up and said, " it was always likely to look well; for everything was nearly new." The officer said,

"But they are clean, and laid out in good order." I would
have rather the officer had not said anything, for it made some
of the old soldiers very surly with me; though others would
give me good advice, and would show me how to do anything.
I gave them a bit of tobacco, or a pint of ale now and then.
Altogether, I got on very well; for if I had enemies I had
friends. I was dismissed from drill in three months, and was
sent from Salford barracks to join my company at Tibb street;
and a good character was sent from Captain Baines to my
captain (Robyns) by the corporal who took me to my company.
I now commenced my duty as a soldier, and I was very contented.

At this time Ireland was in a very disturbed state. On the
6th of June, 1844, we had the route for Ireland. We went by
train to Liverpool. There were six companies of us. On the
morning of the 8th, we went on board the *Rhadamanthus* steam-
ship and set sail for Dublin. We did not land till about 10
o'clock on the 9th, at Kingstown. We then went by railway
to Dublin, and then marched to Richmond barracks, where we
were quartered.

I liked Ireland very well; but our duty was hard. We had
many field-days in Phœnix Park. While lying at these barracks, one day in March, two men asked the captain to let
them go on furlough; but to one he said, "I cannot recommend
you, for you have not been long out of gaol;" and to the other,
"you have not been back from desertion long, so I cannot
recommend you." We were on parade, and he came to me,
and said, "Ryder, fall out; you have never been on furlough,
have you?" I said, "No." The captain then told me to get
my recommendation made out, and he would sign it: but he
did not wait for me to get it made out, as he did it himself.

Now, if any one had told me that I should have gone on
furlough, an hour before, I could not have believed it; for I
had never thought of such a thing, as I had only been twelve

months a soldier, and only the day before I had sent a letter home to say that I should ask next year for a furlough, not having been long enough yet to get one. I had my furlough signed by the Colonel by 4 o'clock, for six weeks; in fact from the 14th of February to the 3rd of April, 1845.

I set sail that night at ten o'clock from Dublin to Liverpool, and the day but one after I was at home, at Twyford. It was dark when I got home; I opened the door, and went in, to the no small surprise of my father and mother. My poor old mother (as soon as she saw me) fell down on the floor as if she had been shot; and I thought the poor old creature would have died, for she was a long time before she came round. I passed the first part of my time very well, but during the latter I was very unsettled; I was tired of being about, doing nothing. So I was glad when the time came for me to return, and I bade my friends farewell.

I was in Ireland with my regiment in a day or two. Soon after I joined the regiment, we changed quarters. We then went to the Royal Barracks; and on the 31st of May, 1845, we marched from Dublin for Athlone, where we arrived on the 5th of June.

Athlone is a large garrison town, and well fortified. The river Shannon flows close by the barracks. My company occupied the Castle; and while here, Lieut. Mansell's servant fell sick. He took me into his service until his man recovered, which was in about a month. After marching to various places, we were ordered into head-quarters again on the 17th of December. We marched into Athlone on the night of the 18th, very fatigued, for it had been raining all day. After being here a few days, Captain Robyns dismissed his servant for misconduct, and sent for me. I went to him, and was very happy, as he was a good master. In February, my master had leave of absence for two months, and he sent me on furlough. I packed his baggage and started him on the 19th, and I left on the 20th of February, 1846.

It was a long way to home ; but as there was a talk that we were going to India, in consequence of the war with the Sikhs —and in fact we had got orders to make the regiment up to a thousand strong—I thought I had better go, as it would very likely be the last time I should ever see my friends.

I passed my time very pleasantly at home ; but I never told my friends that we were going to India : for I thought it would only put them about, and make them uneasy. Before I had been on furlough a fortnight, I heard of letters being sent to men on leave, to join their regiment forthwith ; and some of the men that had only just got home found a letter there ready for them to return. I received none ; so I did not go back until my time was up, which was on the 3rd of April. I joined my regiment at Fermoy, and found that it was under orders for India. My master joined on the 8th.

We marched from Fermoy to Cork on the 8th of May, and went into quarters for a day or two, to wait for the ships coming from London to take us to India. On the 11th we left Cork, and went down to the Cove in steamers, where we found the ships had arrived, and we embarked. My company (the 4th) and the 5th, went on board the Duchess of Northumberland. The officers were Major Brooks (in command), Capt. Robyns, Capt. Pigott, Lieut. Wear, Ensign Turner, and Surgeon Scott ; 200 men, 24 women, and 28 children were also on board. We did not sail till the morning of the 13th, when four ships started together, with a fair wind ; and we bade adieu to " Old Ireland," and also to " Old England," not one half of us ever to see either again.

I here give a short account of the voyage to India. As we sailed from the Cove, all on board stood earnestly watching the land, until we got far out to sea, and all was lost to sight but the wide waters. The two first days we had middling weather. The ship rode along beautifully, making way fast ; but on the morning of the 15th we had reached the Bay of

Biscay, and it was very rough. The sea ran high. It was an awful sight between decks, for nearly all the men and women were sea-sick.

On the 23rd we sailed by the island of Madeira, but not in sight from the decks. On the 26th we passed the Canary Island though not in sight. Here we saw a great quantity of flying fish, and porpoises.

On the 8th of June, we saw a shark round the ship. One man on board was ill of fever. On the 15th we crossed the line at 5, a.m. On the 23rd we saw a whale, within a very short distance of the ship. On the 28th, the sea was very rough; the waves ran high, and swept over our decks like mountains. The women and children, and some of the men, were very frightened. On the 29th, a man died of fever, and on the next day he was cast overboard. The prayers read were those appointed for the dead at sea. We had a very heavy storm in the afternoon, which carried away a number of our sails, and the sea again ran mountains high.

On July the 18th, we were off the Cape of Good Hope. On the 6th of August, a man fell overboard; he was saved by a rope being thrown to him; it was about 8 o'clock in the evening, but it was moonlight, and we were not going more than three or four miles an hour, so that he was easily saved. We lost several men, with a woman and child, from fever, during the voyage.

On the 16th of August a dreadful storm arose suddenly, before we had time to get the sails down. It carried away most of our rigging, and the violence of the waves washed away part of the bulwarks; the ropes breaking and sails flying, as the storm tore them away. The ship tossed about as the waves broke over and swept the decks; and the howling of the wind and roaring of the sea, with the screaming of the women, as they clung around their husbands, were fearful. Some of our younger men began to pray. One man was heard

B

to cry out, "Oh, my poor mother." The storm raged with great violence for about six hours.

On the 19th we were in the Bay of Bengal; and on the 25th we saw land for the first time since we left Cork. On the following day we arrived at the Sand Heads, at the mouth of the river Hoogley, and the day after a pilot came on board. We then entered the river, and could see land on both sides. A boat came alongside us, and our women were frightened at the natives in it; they wear no clothes, except a bit of cloth round the middle of the body. I thought they looked more like monkies than men, and jabbered about the same. On the 28th we came in sight of Calcutta and Fort William.

Calcutta looks from the ship like an English town. It has a very fine appearance. I saw a great number of dead bodies floating down the river by our ship. They were all natives, and birds sat pecking them as they floated.

We could buy everything very cheap, for there were plenty of boats around us. We disembarked on the 31st, and went afterwards up the river, on steamers, to Chinchurrah, where we arrived at 2 o'clock, and then landed. Our men were like madmen; they were so overjoyed at getting on land once more. We were one hundred and nine days on board. I was like a bird let loose from a cage; but the weather was so hot, that we felt it unpleasant, and we were almost worried with musquitoes.

CHAPTER II.

Chinchurrah is a fine station, with very good barracks; it is a receiving depôt for troops landing from England. A great many pensioners and merchants have settled in it. It contains some fine buildings; among others, a college for the natives (who are taught English), some good scholars being turned out of it—a Baptist missionary establishment and a beautiful chapel and school—and a church for the station, upon the river side, close to the officers' quarters. The latter has been standing upwards of two hundred years. It was built by the Dutch, before the English had any possessions in the country. This was their chief settlement. There are also some fine gardens and lovely walks.

We had not been here long, before death began to make sad havoc in the regiment, amongst men, women, and children. This time of the year is very bad for Europeans landing from Europe; for it is the rainy season—consequently, the ground is covered with water; and the damp strikes through every thing. The walls of the barracks were covered with drops of water, and clothes in the boxes required to be taken out and dried. Even the brass on our accoutrements turned yellow in ten minutes after it had been cleaned.

We had been here but about a week, when one night I and a companion were at the canteen, enjoying ourselves with a bottle of ale, and talking over the events of our voyage (for he did not come in the same ship as I did). We parted at nine o'clock to go to bed. He appeared to be in as good health as ever he was; but he was taken with a violent cramp in the stomach and legs, and the eyes and finger-nails turned black. This was about eleven o'clock : he was dead by one o'clock.   My pay-sergeant's wife also died in the same way.   She was a fine-looking young woman, and the mother of two pretty children.   They both died shortly after.   Four or five of our men were bathing on the same day, when as one of them was swimming he suddenly disappeared under the water, and it was concluded by the whole party that an alligator had caught him, and he was put in our regiment orders as drowned, and would be struck off the strength of the regiment ; but it is since proved that he was taken up in England as a deserter.

We buried our dead at night, and such a grave-yard I never witnessed.   The earth being so full of water, it filled the graves immediately; so that we had to pile the earth and stones upon the coffin to sink it.   This was sufficient to give one the horrors.   It is a large grave-yard, and very full now.   At last I was obliged to go to hospital with the bowel complaint.   This is brought on by the dampness of the ground, and eating too much fruit. Great numbers began to die very suddenly from cholera.   The regiment not being used to the like of this, the whole began to look melancholy, and fear was seen on every face, as much as to say, " it will be my turn next."   Some gave themselves up to utter despair and died.   I was very low in spirits myself once, and the more so because I had never been confined to a sick bed in my life.   It was dreadful to see fine, stout, healthy young fellows, well and dead in a few hours ; ah, even before they had time to call on their God !   The good minister was very attentive to the sick, and the Baptist missionary, too. They would bring good books and distribute among the suffer-ers.   Not a day passed but we had some one to put in his last resting-place.   Oh, how often did I wish myself in my native country again ; or that I had died when young.   I accused myself of being an ungrateful wretch, who deserved no better than what he now suffered, for not obeying his old parents. I now felt completely lost, and did not care what became of me.

By degrees I got better, and came out, and never did l feel more pleasure in leaving any place before, as I did in leaving the hospital. Whilst I was in I saw some very sad cases of drunkenness. I believe that some of them drank to drown their sorrow; for I have heard men curse the country and everything in it, to an awful degree, and then they would go to the canteen to get drunk and banish their griefs. The torment that a man had to bear through the day was enough to drive one mad. Thousands upon thousands of flies would be continually buzzing about us, so that one had sufficient to do to keep them off, and if one's mouth was open, they would soon fill it, with a great many other insects. At night there would be hundreds of jackalls, howling and making the most horrible noise I ever heard. We were frightened at first, but we got used to them. Our men would call them the Indian devils, come for some other poor fellow. Then there was the chirping of the crickets and squeaking of frogs, especially in the wet season. Some of the frogs were nearly as big as a man's foot, and they made a noise like a goat bleating.

By the first of October we had lost a great number of men, women, and children, and my complaint came on me again worse than ever. I had not been in the hospital more than eight days, before I was a complete skeleton. The doctor asked me how I felt? I told him .very bad. He shook his head, and then ordered me to be salivated. This was the last remedy he could give; and that would either kill or cure me very quickly; but it had the better effect—for in a few days I began to regain my spirits and to gather strength. My mouth was very sore, my teeth ready to fall out of my head, my tongue swollen too large for my mouth, and my hair came off my head. Still I kept getting strong, and on the 6th of Nov., I was ready to go out to my duty. At last, on the 10th, the doctor discharged me, and never did I feel such a happy release.

We had the General's inspection, and he told us we were going to Agra. The rainy season was now over, and tents and all things ready for the march began to arrive. Our women and sick embarked in the boats, to go towards the place of our destination. We lost upwards of a hundred men, women, and children while we lay at the station. Glad was the whole regiment to get out of this graveyard. We lay in the station two months and twenty days.

On the 20th of November, at half-past 4 o'clock, we marched out of Chinchurrah. It was a beautiful morning. The stars shone bright and clear. As we marched through the town, the natives were squatted upon their housetops to see us pass along, and hear the band play, which had struck up the tune, "Should old acquaintance be forgot." We bounded along with light hearts, and were glad to get away from a place where so many of our countrymen were left in their graves. The road was pretty good, and we passed along a very fine part of the country. The fine topes of cocoa-nut, and lemon, and banyan trees gave a delightful appearance to it; and especially the large banyan tree, with its wide-spreading boughs. We left the river Hoogley on our right. We passed a great deal of corn, and rice and sugar plantations.

We arrived at our camp at 8 o'clock. The ground that our tents were pitched on was rather rough. We had a great many camp followers with us, for different purposes; some to carry water, others to look after the tents, others to cook, some to sweep the ground to pitch the tents upon, shoeblacks, barbers, washermen, and a portion of merchants selling things; in fact, there are as many natives with a regiment on the line of march as there are men. Our baggage was carried in a rude kind of cart, called an "accry," drawn by a yoke of oxen, and some by two, according to the size of the "accry."

We halted on the 21st, for the purpose of giving time for the commissariat to come up with grog and flour, tea and coffee, and sugar, and other necessary supplies. A man was flogged for being drunk on the line of march. A native soldier, a "sepoy," also died. A guard attends every European regiment on the march, in attendance on the commissariat department and orderlies.

On the 24th we came up to the town of Birdwan. This is the place where a native prince lives. He was educated in England. We saw here a great many European houses, with beautiful gardens round them. We passed by the seat of the prince. He stood at the gate to look at us. He wore a green silk velvet dress, and a large gold belt round his shoulder, hanging down on the left side. He was a fine-looking man, with handsome features, apparently about 26 years of age, and of the middle stature; he was very smart and clever. He spoke the best of English, and appeared very cheerful. He had a European lady upon his arm, and several gentlemen in attendance, with a large number of native officers and a guard.

As we marched through the town, I observed that every house was neat and clean, with a small garden in front, laid out in the English style. The people appeared very obliging, and a number of boys and some of the men could speak good English. There are a church and chapel, and a school, in which to teach both the native and the English languages, with a missionary establishment, and schoolmasters and mistresses. There is a jail, and a good zoological garden, with a collection of wild animals.

The prince inspected our camp in the evening. He chatted with our officers quite freely. He invited them all to dine with him at his palace, which is a very splendid place. I went into the town and saw a number of Christian natives.

We struck camp at 3 o'clock on the 25th, and passed over a beautiful part of the country. We pitched camp at 8 o'clock.

Two men died in the evening: one of them belonged to my company. He marched in to camp with the company and appeared as well as usual; but he was dead by 4 o'clock. We buried the men at sunset. We dug a grave with our bayonets as well as we could, having first sewed the bodies up in thick pieces of cloth, which served for coffins.

We struck camp at the usual hour, on the 26th, and we passed thickly-inhabited villages. They are built of mud or sun-burnt clay. A few brick buildings, where their richer inhabitants live, may be seen; and their temples or places of worship, which are always built of brick, and plastered over, and whitewashed, and adorned with figures of different animals, such as snakes, monkies, tigers, peacocks, and so on; but they are very rudely painted.

We paraded at 4 o'clock on the 28th, and marched over a wild uncultivated piece of country, and crossed a chain bridge —a very splendid one, too. It was erected over a large water-course by the East India Company. When we pitched camp, the wild beasts were howling round us all night.

The following day being Sunday, we halted, and our colonel read the church prayers.

On the first of December we marched over a wild, mountainous part of the country. Many wild beasts—tigers, bears, hyenas, and monkeys—were quite common. We passed over a third chain bridge. It is a curious thing to notice, but the elephants will not walk over these bridges; they will go through the bed of the river or through the water. They will beat them with their trunks, and if the least shaking is felt, they will not proceed along them, nor will any coaxing make them.

On the 2nd, we came up to a river at day-break; it was half a mile across, including the bed on each side, which is about two hundred yards, of very heavy sand. We had to ford it; it took us up to our middles. We were obliged to go in the rear of the accrys, and push them through the sand. With this delay we did not get away from the river until the sun was very hot, and then we had five miles to go, on a very bad road, and all jungle on each side. Our colonel had the kindness to send us a glass of grog a man. We walked as fast as ever we could, and reached camp at 11 o'clock, faint and exhausted.

The part of the country in which we were on the 7th was very full of jungle; and the wild beasts were very dangerous. At daylight, two tigers crossed the road, in front of the advance-guard. We pitched camp at 8 o'clock. One of our bullocks was sprung upon by a tiger, in the evening, about dusk; it tore a large piece of flesh out of the bullock's side, but did not kill it. Some of our recruits became so alarmed at the wild beasts, that they dare not stop on sentry at night. It was very dangerous to be alone in the jungle, when from the darkness of the night you could not see a yard beyond you; but we enlist to face dangers.

As we proceeded the road was very sandy, which raised such a cloud of dust that it was very diffcult to breathe. We could not see five yards in our front; and through the sweat on our faces, and the sand settling on us, we were nearly as black as natives.

We came on the 12th to a small encampment, which proved to be the late king of Lahore's. He was a prisoner, having been taken in the late campaign of the Sutlej. He came to see us march into and pitch our camp; he was a fine looking man, very stout. Next day (being Sunday) our officers invited the king to the camp, and my company paraded as a guard of honour. He inspected the camp very closely. He would not eat or drink with us on account of his religion, which teaches that our food is unclean and would pollute the Hindoos.

Nothing particular occurred until we struck camp on the 21st, for the purpose of fording a river. We marched across, and left our arms and accoutrements and jackets with the guard;

C

and then went to drag the baggage over, and get it through
the water. It took us up to the arm-pits. We had not got it
all over until 6 o'clock, when we were very hungry and tired.
The heat of the sun was intolerable. We had two or three
accrys fast in the quicksand; and when we crossed, the water
was very difficult to stand in; for the sand under our feet was
continually shifting. The current was so strong that one man
was taken away, and all we could do we could not save him.
Two days are allowed for crossing this river; but we exerted
ourselves, so that we had done by night. Our colonel gave us
an extra allowance of grog, and allowed us a halt, to rest ourselves and dry our tents and clothes, which we stood greatly in
need of. He gave us great credit for our exertions in making
the passage of the river so quickly.

At sunrise, on the 24th, we came up to a very good-looking
town, very thickly encircled with fruit trees and vineyards. It
looked like an ancient place. We formed our camp round the
ruins of an old castle. It had once been very strongly fortified.
Some of the architecture was still standing; the stones were
carved in the old style. The place was completely surrounded
by a tank of water, about a hundred yards across; and it could
only be approached by a narrow bridge. We received a fresh
route this day; we were to march to Meerut.

The next being Christmas-day, we all had a double allowance
of grog and rations served out. We went to the village, and
bought some young pigs, and roasted them. I received a
letter from home, with a ribbon in it as a keepsake.

On the 28th, we passed over another chain-bridge. It was
the most splendid bridge I saw in the country. It was built at
the expense of the rajah. It crossed the river Cavendish, the
water of which is believed to be holy; and numbers of the
natives come to bathe and bless themselves in it.

On the day following we marched over a beautiful part of the
country, and passed a fine idol at a temple. At daylight,

on the 30th, we came up to the river Ganges, and crossed
by a bridge of boats. The river is about half a mile across,
with a very strong current. We got over without any accident,
but the elephants would not go on the bridge—they swam
through the water. The city of Benares is on the opposite
bank ; it is an ancient city, and a great many European merchants live in it, on account of the river being navigable down
to Calcutta. It put me in mind of England more than any
other place. There were all kinds of English vegetables and
goods for merchandise. The general and a large number of
officers came to meet us. Three infantry regiments, and cavalry
and artillery, were stationed there—all natives. Some volunteers joined us here, from the 39th regiment.

On the last day of the old year, we halted at Benares. Our
officers played a game of cricket against the officers of the
sepoys, which was continued the next day.

Our daily marches were continued, and on the 7th we pitched
our camp on the main river Ganges. The city of Allehabad
was on the opposite bank, about three miles from our camp.
A great many natives came to us, with all sorts of provisions, and a number of volunteers came over to see their new
regiment.

On the following day we passed through Allehabad. It
is a fine old city. A great number of Europeans live there.
A large garrison of native troops and European artillery always
lie there. It is a receiving depôt, for recruits for regiments
stationed up the country.

A great number of pilgrims were encamped about ; they
come for thousands of miles on a pilgrimage to this place, in
order to bathe in the river. Here is the meeting of the waters
of two rivers, which the superstition of the natives leads them
to think are holy ; and that after they have bathed in them
and drunk them their sins are forgiven. They carry the water
away with them, and so long as they have any of it in their

possession, when any one of their family is dying, they pour a
drop of it in their mouths, believing they will then die in confidence of heaven. They have to pay very dearly for the water.
There is also a tree, called the "bleeding tree of Allehabad."
The natives have great superstition about it; but they are
most grossly imposed upon by their padres, or parsons, who
can make them believe anything; for the tree is nothing more
than a post with a hole in it, where they put some kind of stuff
in to make the natives believe it is blood.

The volunteers joined us this afternoon; some from the 50th
regiment, and some from the 39th. The 14th regiment, native
infantry, entered our camp on the morning of the 17th. They
were escorting the Lahore tribute money down the country.
They are a fine-looking regiment. They were engaged in the
late war with the Sikhs.

On the 20th we met the 62nd regiment at daylight. Being
the youngest regiment, they payed us the compliment of a
salute. They were not very strong; they gave a great many
volunteers to different regiments. They were *en route* to Calcutta, there to embark for England; and many a time did I
wish to be with them.

At sunrise we came in sight of Cawnpore—a large military
station. We approached the line of the cavalry, which was
out on parade, and we were met by a large body of officers.
There were here European and native artillery, and two
regiments of native cavalry, and three regiments of native
infantry. It is a station for European cavalry and infantry.
It is a beautiful place, containing a large number of European
inhabitants, and all kinds of trade are carried on in it. Some
splendid houses, with large gardens and vineyards, are here
to be seen. I saw also a coach-maker's shop, and several
watch-makers, and other traders. We marched by a church,
—a very splendid one, too; it had a spire upon it, and a clock.
It put me in mind of home. Our women met us here, as the

river comes up to the place. There was great rejoicing when
they met us, but two of them had to weep, for their husbands
were buried on the march; several women and children had
also been buried coming up the river. Our camp was soon
filled with plenty of every kind of provisions. The cause of
this being a large military post is, that the Nepaul country comes
up to within a short distance of this station, and the
king has been rather hostile to the British power, although he
pays tribute to our government; so that a few troops lying
here keep him in check.

I visited the grave-yard on the 22nd; it was close to our camp,
and is full of my fellow-countrymen. A great number of very
fine monuments are erected over the bodies. I observed great
numbers of the 3rd regiment, or "Old Buffs," and the 14th
regiment, and the 11th and 8th light dragoons (now hussars).

Everything being ready, we marched on the morning of the
23rd; our women having started on the previous evening. We
had rain all night on the 26th, and our tents were very wet
and heavy and uncomfortable, so that it was feared the cattle
could not carry them; but as our cooks and commissariat went
on the night before, we were obliged to go or have nothing to
eat. As it cleared up a little, we started, though the rain
soon fell very heavily all the way; so that we had not a dry thread
upon us. When we pitched our tents we had nowhere to sit
down, nor lay our things, except upon the ground; and it was
swimming with water. As we halted next day, to dry our tents
and bedding and clothing, I took a ramble into the country,
and a beautiful one it was. The corn and tobacco and indigo
were looking very well. I visited some gardens, and got some
fruit. We could see the ruins of an ancient city, which had
once been large and flourishing.

On the morning of the 29th, we met the 50th regiment on its
way to Calcutta, there to embark for England. It was not
very strong; it was an unlucky regiment. It was engaged in

all the late wars, and after that, the barracks, of Loodianah fell
upon it, and killed a great number more; and some years
before, as it was coming up the country in boats, the men were
wrecked upon the river Ganges.

After several days' marching we came up to the city of
Allagur, just as it was getting dusk. It is a fine large place,
and is the greatest resort in India for European planters.
Different other trades are carried on there; and it is the residence of a number of pensioners.

On the morning of the 12th of February, I visited an old
graveyard, which proved to be the place where the dead were
buried who fell at the taking of Allagur some years ago. Here
is a monument erected to the memory of the honourable dead.

On Sunday, the 14th, just as we had finished prayers, a
dreadful thunder-storm came on. The thunder and lightning
were terrific, and the rain fell in a complete sheet of water.
Such a storm I never saw before. Everything was soon wet
through; but it cleared up at 2 o'clock in the afternoon. The
storm commenced again at 8 o'clock in a frightful manner,
when it was pitch dark. I was on guard at the time. The
storm tore down several of our tents, and even trees. We had
not a dry thread on us, and none to put on. The storm cleared
up towards morning, and it turned out a fine day. We halted
to dry our tents and clothes; our baggage went on to Meerut
under a guard.

In the evening of the 18th we paraded, in order to see that
everything was clean to march into Meerut with in the morning.
Our colonel said he was surprised to see us so clean—we looked
as though we had turned out of barracks instead of having
just finished a long and tedious march. We struck camp at 5
o'clock, on the 19th, for the last time before reaching Meerut,
and glad we were; so we tripped along, and thought nothing
of the distance. My company was the advance guard. A
large number of officers and inhabitants came to meet us, as

we got near the town. All the volunteers also came, to see their new regiment march in. We did not notice much of the town, for the road did not lead to it; but it is a large place and thickly inhabited by natives and Europeans. The barracks are on the east side of the town, about a mile from it, on a large common. We got to them about 6 o'clock, and formed line for the general to inspect us. He said that we were a fine young regiment, and very clean. When we were dismissed, the men of the 80th regiment came and invited us to breakfast. They had prepared one on purpose, and a very good one, too, with the addition of a dram of grog per man. This was very kind of that noble regiment. They were in the same barracks as we. The 9th lancers were a short distance on our left, and the artillery on the right; there were also three native regiments. It was a most splendid-looking station. The church was close to our barracks—a very fine one, too. This was the end of a long and tedious march of three months, and a thousand miles.

CHAPTER III.

MEERUT is a fine military station, and contains a large number of European and native merchants, who carry on a good business in European merchandise. The officers' quarters are pleasantly situated, with fine gardens round them. The country all round Meerut is well-cultivated, and contains numerous villages. There is a large grave-yard here, full of graves, with some beautiful monuments. Two splendid ones are erected over the remains of general officers; and we had not been here long before we began to lay some of our comrades in the same place, though we had pretty good health in general.

Here is a play-house, in which our officers and men got up some very good plays. There is also a catholic chapel, and another for the use of the dissenting soldiers. There are a native and a missionary to preach to and teach them all. The minister also preaches at the dissenters' chapel. About seven miles from here is a place called Sodanah, where is a large Roman Catholic college and chapel, for Europeans and natives. It is a very splendid one; it was built at the expense of a native queen.

When the hot season set in, we were tormented to death (as it were) with bugs; they were in our cots by thousands. Very seldom could we sleep upon our cots at night. We would take our bed and lay it upon the ground, out in the open air. This was the only way we could get a bit of rest.

When the day approached, the heat would be so excessive, that no one dare venture out for fear of being struck by the sun. We had several killed by it, and in the barracks we would be so hot, that it would be torture to be there. The sweat would come through everything we had upon us; in fact we could have nothing on but a thin pair of drawers, with no shirt; and the millions of flies that would be continually tormenting us would be sufficient to drive men mad. When getting our victuals our plates were black over with the flies. We were obliged to eat with one hand and buffet them away with the other. I have often heard our men curse their God; and they would get as much money as they could, and then go and get so drunk they could not speak. They would often say that was the only way they could have any peace: but I could not see any pleasure in such a way. I have seen men die in this state, and others drown themselves, or shoot themselves, whilst a number lose their senses and die raving mad—in fact, half the deaths in this country are caused by drink. I hated the country: it grew worse and worse every day. The only exercise I could take was to walk two miles every night, after sunset, across the plains. The hot wind was dreadful. We had several men transported for striking non-commissioned officers; and as the crime was getting worse in the country, the Commander-in-chief warned the soldiers in a General Order that he should be obliged to carry the military law into execution in full force if the crime did not cease.

The rainy season set in about the latter part of July. It cooled the air a little, but it was very close and sultry. I bought a fowling-piece to enjoy myself in shooting. I and my comrade had several fine rambles, and we shot as much game as we could carry. In the beginning of September we started out on a shooting excursion, and had a pretty good forenoon in the topes of trees and sugar plantations, when my comrade and I parted. I went over to a tope of trees at a distance away, whilst he stopped about the place he was at; and when he was going round the trees and looking

D

in them, he fell down a well—powder, shot, gun, and game,
altogether. Had it not been for the natives he never would
have got out again; for the well was deep, and had a large
quantity of water in it. He was dragged up by the natives
with some ropes, and then one of them got up the gun. I came
back to the place where I left him; and on seeing him I asked
him what had been the matter. He then told me. We gave
the men who had got him up a present, and proceeded home;
but the next day I found myself very bad with a fever, through
going so much in the sun the previous day. The day following
I was obliged to go to hospital, and became very ill. My head
was shaved and blistered twice, and 132 leeches put upon my
temples. My case was doubtful for some time; but I gradually recovered.

At this time the rainy season was over, and the cold season
began to set in. Our officers had returned from the snowy
range of mountains, when something worse happened, which
I have to relate in this place.

On arriving at Meerut we received a number of volunteers
from other regiments which were going to England, and it was
remarked by many, that after these volunteers joined us, a great
deal of drunkenness was witnessed in the regiment. The new
comers appeared to lead our men off, and through their getting
connected together, drunkenness and mutinous conduct commenced to a fearful extent, forty men having been transported
within a few months, and many others having been differently
dealt with, as by imprisonment and flogging. This had all
taken place in this station and one or two others near it; but
the most of it in ours.

The Commander-in-chief had repeatedly warned the men by
General Orders, cautioning them that striking superior officers
was punishable by death, and that he should be compelled to
carry it into execution, if the crime was not put a stop to. The

commanding officers of the regiment had done all in their power to impress it upon the men's minds that the extremity of the law would certainly be carried out, and that before long some one would die for his folly. I saw our Colonel, when he had formed us into a square, sit upon his horse, cautioning the men until the tears ran down his face on to the horse's neck. He was our second Colonel, and was well liked by all. He was very severe where severity was required. His name was Hill. He had been all his time in the regiment, but left us shortly after, and went to the 21st regiment.

Not long after this a man was tried and sentenced to death, but was recommended for mercy on account of his previous good character. He got off with transportation, the Commander-in-chief being still unwilling to put a man to death.

Before many more days had passed over, four more came before him. One was a man of the artillery, who struck the doctor while in hospital. Another was a man of the 9th Lancers, who had struck the commanding officer in the face with his cap. The third was a man of my regiment, accused of striking a sergeant whilst he was being tried by a district court-martial. The fourth was a man of the 80th regiment; but what his crime was I do not know, as the regiment marched down the country after the first execution, and this man got off with being transported for life.

The first of these men was shot. It was the artilleryman. I have forgotten his name; and, as I did not see the execution take place, I cannot say much about it, except that he did not believe that he should be shot. He thought that he should at the last moment get his reprieve, for he believed he was sentenced for an example. He was executed at sun-rise. I was in hospital at the time, being nearly recovered from the sun-stroke. I heard the fatal shots fired. I came out of hospital the next day; and on Sunday, at church, the station minister preached a

very touching sermon on the matter. He said that he had
visited the man in his cell, and was with him night and day,
but he could make no impression upon his mind as to his fate,
nor prevail on him to prepare for another world. The minister
believed that he died totally unprepared to meet his God. He
came from Manchester, and was of respectable parents.

The next case was that of a man of the 9th Lancers. I saw
this, and can tell more about it. It was early in the morning,
before daylight, that we paraded for the execution, and formed
in three sides of a square, the open side being left for the balls
to pass through, when the soldiers fired. The unhappy man was
then brought from his cell, under an escort of a section of
men, commanded by an officer, his arms being tied behind him
by a cord a little above the elbow, so that his hands were in
some degree at liberty. He was taken to the left of the square,
next to his own regiment, for it was not yet day-break. We
all stood silent and sorrowful, waiting for the first dawn of the
morning. Every thing was so still that a pin might be heard
to fall. I stood trembling all over, until I could not keep a
limb still—my teeth chattered in my mouth; but this was
greatly owing to weakness, as I had but just come from hospital.
However, several fainted, and others had to fall out. Day soon
broke. After the first dawn I could see the party stand with
the prisoner, when they were ordered to proceed in the following
manner: first the provost with his arms reversed; then the band
and drummers, playing the " Dead March," the drums being
muffled with black; next the firing party, with arms reversed;
then the coffin, borne by four men; next to this the prisoner,
in company of the minister praying, and his comrade on the left
of him, flanked by a man on either side with swords, the escort
following. They started from the left; the band played the
dismal and solemn march, which made my blood run cold. As
he passed his own regiment, he bade his officers and the men

farewell, and told them he hoped it would be a warning to all
to keep from drink; for it was that and bad company that had
brought him to this. He saluted his colours as he passed them.
When they got up to my regiment, I looked at him. He was
pale, though he appeared to be prepared for his fate, which I
suppose he was. The minister had hold of his arm, but he
walked with a firm step, keeping the step to the drum, and
with the party. He was dressed in a clean white shirt, a black
handkerchief, his stable jacket (with the coller turned back),
white trowsers, and stable cap. As soon as he got to us, he
began to weep, and was going to say something; but the
minister spoke to him, and I suppose told him to continue in
prayer. Poor man! I thought my heart would melt in me,
when I saw him so close to me; as I was up in the front.
Several men being unable to stand it, they had fallen to the
rear. As he passed our colonel and colours, he saluted them,
and bade all farewell. On getting to the end of the square,
they turned across to the open side, about the middle, and
the coffin was put on the ground. The escort fell back; the
firing party took up their distance; the man knelt upon his
coffin; the provost blufted him, and then drew back; the
minister read the funeral service; the man prayed; as the
minister finished, he said, " Lord, have mercy upon my soul!"
and the minister, putting up his hand as a signal that all was
finished, the report of the muskets was heard as they poured
out a volume of smoke, and the man fell dead. Two balls had
passed through the heart, one through the breast, another
through the head, and another through the thigh. After the
whole of us had marched by the body, it was put in the coffin
as it fell, and buried.

On the morning of the 28th we paraded, as on the previous
day, to witness another military execution. This was a man of
my regiment. His name was Jurden, and he was an Irishman

and a volunteer. His offence was striking a sergeant; but
what his reason was for doing so, I do not know. He said he
wanted to get transported. He did this before the other men
were executed. Everything was carried on at this as on the
other occasions, except that this man was a Catholic, and was
attended by the priest. He did not walk so firmly as the other
men; he reeled several times; and I believe he would have
fallen had he not been supported by the priest and his comrades. He fell pierced by seven balls through the body.
When he was informed that he was to be shot, he wept bitterly.
His cries were enough to melt the heart of the stones of his
cell, had it been possible. He had seen the other two men
shot, as all the prisoners were marched up to the place in order
to witness the execution.

This example had the desired effect, for we had no more
striking superior officers. The punishment for striking is very
severe, and some people do not hold with it; but such must be
the case while the British army is composed of such a set of
men as it is, of all characters and dispositions, or discipline
would never be kept.

On the 27th of December, 1847, my master went to England,
for the purpose of selling out of the service. I felt very uneasy
and disturbed in my mind with the thoughts of his leaving.
Many a time did I wish I was again with him. I had been
with him two years, and always found him a kind-hearted
gentleman; and I must say I felt proud of being servant to
such a man. He was tasteful, and always liked everything
to be clean about him: he gave me a very handsome present
when he left; and during the time I was with him, we never
had an angry word.

On February the 13th, 1848, I was appointed lance corporal, in
the light company into which I had been transferred, and on
the 14th we marched to Umballah. We had a very good

march: the fields and everything were pleasant and green. Fine crops of corn were to be seen. On the 16th, we pitched our camp on the banks of the river Hindoo. It is not very large. We saw several fine tortoises in it. It is crossed by a chain bridge—a very fine one, too.

From this we could see the towers of the city of Delhi, the largest, oldest, and richest in India.

On the 17th, we struck camp at 4 o'clock, and, as we drew nearer, daylight broke in, and as fine a morning as ever opened on any regiment. As we went along, we passed some beautiful gardens and buildings, and a water-mill—the first I ever saw in India, or ever heard tell of. It was built by, or under the instructions of, some British engineers.

By this time the sun had begun to rise, and to shine on the lofty towers and domes, with their gilt tops, which gave a grand and noble appearance to them. They looked as if they were of gold, and in fact they put me in mind of the enchanted cities I had read of in books. Before we got to the town we had to cross a river by a bridge of boats. On both sides was a large bed of sand, and a stream of water runs round this side of the walls. The city never could be taken on this side; for the river is a good defence. As we entered, there was a guard of boys dressed in uniform, who, I learnt, belonged to the king. He was training them to the British discipline.

Delhi is a very clean place, and contains a great number of large shops. The main streets are very wide, with a row of trees up the centre, so that they form a good shade from the sun. A great number of the king's officers came to see us enter. They were very richly dressed, and the horses and elephants they rode were splendidly ornamented. I saw some of the finest Arab horses here ever eye rested upon.

We marched by the palace; it is inside the city, and a large stone wall and ditch lie all round. We only saw the outside;

but it is a splendid building. We pitched our camp on the Lahore side, within 100 yards of the gate, and by the border of some gardens.   No European troops lie there but artillery. There are four or five regiments of native infantry, and cavalry. The largest arsenal and magazines are kept here.   The city is defended on this side by a large stone wall and ditch.

This place was never taken by the British, but surrendered after a hard-fought battle, within a few miles of the city.   It is the seat of the Great Mogul's empire.   He ruled all India, or nearly so, at one time ; and the natives believe that he stands between God and man.   Since the conquest by the British, his power is nothing : he is merely the temporary chief of the city, but that is under the British authority.

My comrade and self visited the city in the afternoon. As we walked along the streets, we saw all kinds of stones for sale in quantities, such as diamonds, rubies, crystals, cornelians, garnets, and various others, all cut in different shapes, ready to be set in ornaments.   I bought a few to keep.   We next went to the gold market, where we saw some splendid rings, pins, bracelets, ear-rings, and sundry other things, set with stone ; also, good lace of all patterns.   We then got into the cloth-market, where some fine silk shawls, scarfs, and other things, too numerous to mention, were exposed for sale. Afterwards we saw a quantity of large looking-glasses.   We next went to the Temple Royal, or the church, where the king goes to prayer.   It is a large square building, with towers at each corner.   We had to go up about sixty steps to get to the gates, which are of brass, and very large.   They open both ways, half each way.   They are of the size of a pair of barn-doors.   When we got to the top of the steps, at the gates, we were requested to take off our shoes before we could be allowed to go in ; but we refused to do so—for, as we thought, it would be like bowing to an idol.   For this reason we did not go in: we could see as we stood at the gate that the building in the inside was of marble, and the floor too. The court is square, and about one hundred yards across, with a large tank in the centre, full of water, and several flowing fountains. We could see some of their images that they pray to; but as we did not go in, we could not say any more about the temple. Some of our men took off their shoes: they went in, and they gave a good account of the building.

A number of Europeans, in government employ, live outside the city. We saw a missionary and his son: they lived in the town. There was a Baptist chapel; the missionary's name was Thomson. A school is established for the natives, and we saw several who could read and write English far better than I could. When we returned to camp, I was very tired, after such a long ramble, and a long day's march.

On the 18th we halted, and again visited the city, for the purpose of going to see the Palace; but as some of our men told us that we should have to take off our shoes, we would not go. I believe it is a splendid place, built of marble.

On the 19th we marched, and passed by many gardens. Some of them were very large, reaching for miles in length. We pitched our camp on a beautiful part of the country; it is surrounded by corn, as far as the eye can reach.

On the 24th we reached Kurnaul—a large town. It was also a large military station for European and native troops; but on account of being so unhealthy it was abandoned in 1844. This place is famous for the good European boots made in it. We pitched our camp upon the plain, near to the church and the old barracks. They are entirely in ruins now, in this short time. The houses for the officers' quarters were some of the finest I ever saw in India. This was a stirring place at one time; but any person would think, to look at it now, that it had been left in ruins for at least fifty years, instead of four only. It is now melancholy and lonely. Two regiments of

E

native infantry, two of native cavalry and native artillery, are
still here. I visited two grave-yards: they were full of dead,
left there and forgotten. I could not help sighing, and feeling
for those who lay sleeping in their graves, with no other trace
left but a solitary stone with their names upon it, to tell who
lay there, far away from their native shores.

We left this place on the 25th, and had a pretty good march
to Umballah. The ground was well cultivated, and looked
very well. We passed through a few small jungles, arriving at
Umballah on the 1st of March. As we approached, we were
met by a number of officers and men of the 3rd light dragoons,
which was lying here. The barracks (each holding a company)
are built of sun-burnt bricks, and are not very comfortable.
They stand , upon a plain; the artillery and third regiment of
light dragoons being on our right, and three regiments of
native infantry and cavalry on our left. This station was built
in 1845, and is only a poor place yet, though it is healthy, and
will be a large station in time. We could see the Himalaya
mountains very plainly from here. They appeared to be close
to us on a clear day, and looked very grand, with their towering
tops covered with snow, far above the clouds.

While here I made application for my discharge; but the war
broke out, and I went no further about it; for our officers were
ordered to join from the hills, which told very plainly that we
were for the field before long; and although it was the hot
season, warlike stores were preparing and moving up the
country. In the beginning of May we were ordered to hold
ourselves in readiness, to march at a moment's notice. We
were all ready and willing, for every one seemed anxious to try
his courage, and assert his colours with honour. All was talk
and bustle, and no one knew where we were for. We were to
be ready by the 14th in light marching order.

CHAPTER IV.

On Sunday, the 14th, we were parading for church prayers at 4, p.m., when orders were received for us to be ready to march at a moment's notice. We were to pack all our baggage up, and put it into store, except a change of clothing; the women and children, and sick and weakly men, to be left behind. All was hurry and bustle and confusion. Bugles were sounding, and non-commissioned officers running in all directions. Sixty rounds of ball-cartridge were served out per man. We paraded at six o'clock, in order that it might be seen that every man was ready. Men and officers were present. Our first colonel, and oldest captain, had not joined us, being upon the hill on leave. The colonel having formed square, and ordered the two officers that carried the colours to the front, spoke as follows :—

" Men and Officers,—you know what this march is for, or we should not march in this season of the year, so hot as it is. I feel proud to have the honour of commanding such a fine body of men. So I now call upon you to do your duty, which I know you will do. I now call upon you to present arms to your colours" (they were already unfurled and waving in the breeze ; and, at the same time pointing to the colours, with tears in his eyes, he continued ;) " men,—I call upon you to present arms to your colours, by which we live and by which we'll die, if required." He then dismissed the parade.

Poor man ! when he said these words, how little did he think that he would be one of the first men who would fall in their defence : he died like a good and gallant man, well respected by all.

Our boxes were now put into store. Camels and elephants began to arrive; and bullocks and accrys (rudely constructed carts) to take our tents and baggage and ammunition.

By 7 o'clock I was all ready for the march. I had a few little keepsakes, which I did not wish to be destroyed if I fell; so I gave them to one of our women, with directions where they should be sent. I then joined the rest of the men, who were lying upon their cots, bitterly thinking upon the march, which we knew would be wearisome at this time of the year, when the heat was at 95 and 100 degrees.

At eight o'clock an order arrived that we were to march at midnight, on the road leading to Ferozepoor. The order spread like wildfire through the regiment. All now was throng and bustle—sergeants and corporals ordering the men to get the tents out of store and loaded; others again, warning the officers. Women were weeping and children crying. The camels were bellowing and elephants roaring, as their loads were put upon them; and the blacks, too, were jabbering. Altogether, it seemed as if Bedlam was let loose.

Twelve o'clock soon arrived, and the bugles rang their shrill notes for dress. We were soon ready, and the parade formed, officers and men being present. Now was the most affecting time for the married men: it was really heart-rending to see the poor women taking their last farewell of their husbands, and some for ever. No more were they to see those moving limbs, nor feel the press of those hands, nor the kiss of those lips; but soon was a ball to pass through that body, and leave it to moulder and decay, or rather, to be torn and made food for wild beasts! I thought it was well to be a single man, to have no such troubles as these.

At about one o'clock the words "quick march" were given, and the band struck up "The girl I left behind me." The morning was very fine, and the moon shone bright; but the air was very sultry, and the sand rose in a cloud as we marched;

so much so that we could scarcely get our breath. The band stopped playing, for the sand rose in such clouds that we could not see the next man to us, at times. At about three o'clock the men began to fall out by sections, from want of water, the heat being nearly unbearable, and their tongues hanging out to a frightful size, and their mouths being parched up. All the cry was for water. At length we came to a well, and all order in the ranks was at an end. What few besthes (water-carriers) we had were soon surrounded, and nearly worried: the men were like madmen, pushing one over another. The strongest got the most—the weakly men praying in a most pitiful manner, and offering all the money they possessed for a drink.

We halted for some time, when order was restored. Our officers did all in their power to get water for us. We marched until about four o'clock, when we came up to another well, and the men were as disorderly at this as at the other; it was very troublesome marching all across loose sand. We pressed guides to conduct us from village to village.

We pitched our camp about seven o'clock, every man being completely beaten up, and their feet so very sore from the extreme heat of the sand. It was so light that we sank up to the ankles. We got nothing to eat until twelve o'clock, as our commissariat had not arrived until late. Our route being so sudden, it gave him no time to get carriages. One of our camp-followers fell dead for want of water. Our camps arrived, with grog, and every man got a dram, of which we stood in great need. One pound of bread was served out per man; so that was all we got, after marching from one o'clock until seven. Our cooks did not arrive until night; and we dare say nothing to them, for fear they would not go any further with us.

The sun and hot winds were dreadful. There we lay, faint and weary, panting for breath. We were paraded at seven o'clock in the evening. A sergeant was tried by a court-martial and reduced. The colonel spoke to the regiment, and said he was surprised to see the men march so well, considering the heat, and our wants being so badly supplied; but that he would press Beasthes (water-carriers) at the villages.

"Beasthes" are men who always accompany troops march-ing, to carry water in skins. They use a goat's skin, tanned whole; so the neck part is where the water goes in and out at. They carry it by a strap passed over one shoulder, the skin hanging upon the hip, with the neck to the front.

We struck camp at 11 o'clock, p.m. Weak and faint, we commenced another dreadful march. The sand rose in clouds as bad as the day previously. We could scarcely get our breath. We had not marched far before we had not a dry thread upon us, the sweat running down into our boots; our eyes and nose and mouth also being nearly stuffed up with sand. It was as bad as being tortured to get our breath. Men began to fall from want of water; nothing but the cry of "water." As the thirst increases, everything has become dreadful. The night is awfully close, and the sand increases the thirst. Men begin to hate one another; the best of friends will fall out;— every man for himself.

We marched until two o'clock, when we came up to the party that had gone on in advance to look for water. They had got some, but it was like a drop of rain falling into the sea; it was drunk up in a minute, the weakest going to the wall; they got little or none. The wells not being far away, we soon made to them, and all round was one mass of men, striving for a drink. The water got very thick and muddy, but no matter —all went down together, as if it was as clear as crystal. After halting here half-an-hour, and the men being satisfied, we proceeded on our march; but it was no little that satisfied us, for I drank two quarts at a draught, and numbers drank more; we seemed as if we should never be satisfied.

We got on pretty well for about an hour, when the cry of "Pawney" (water) was heard, and things began to be as before. We arrived at a well about four o'clock. All was confusion and disorder until all were satisfied. Our officers were refused water, for the men would sooner part with gold; it was to them even more precious. I saw our colonel bidding the officers to stand back, and let the men come first, and he was working hard in drawing up water for the men. He was well beloved by his regiment. He shared everything with his men, and he was willing to fare as his men fared.

I saw a very large tree as we marched by it, A thousand men could easily take shelter under its branches. It was by far the largest I had ever seen. We passed by a funeral pile; the corpse was laid upon it, and all appeared to be ready for lighting.

Marching over a beautiful bridge, built under the superintendence of a British engineer, we arrived at the town of Putallah, the residence of a native prince. It is walled all round, and guns mounted upon it. I saw his troops at drill: fine large men they were. We passed the burial ground, or rather burning ground; for they are all of the Hindoo caste or religion. I saw heaps of human ashes and half-consumed bones. A few women sat mourning by some of the remains of the burnt bodies.

After passing the town we marched through a vine-field about two miles. It was full of all kinds of fruits, such as mango, pomegranate, tamarind, banana, orange, lemon, and all other trees of the native kind. We pitched our camp about seven o'clock by the side of two good wells. So for one blessing we had good water, and we made good use of it, too. I got a good wash, which refreshed me, and made me feel very comfortable. We got our grog served out as soon as we had pitched our camp, but it was six o'clock before we had anything to eat: and when we did get it we could not eat it, for our appetites were gone.

The rajah, or native prince, sent a body of his cavalry to

guard our camp, and promised the colonel to furnish us with camels and elephants, to carry our sick and baggage, and a squadron of cavalry to watch our baggage through his dominions. He gave us leave to press men at villages. He is under the British protection.

On Tuesday we struck camp at half-past eleven o'clock, p.m. We started pretty well, but we had not proceeded far before the sand began to rise as bad as ever, and the men to fall out by sections. We came to a well about two o'clock; but now we were worse off than ever, for our carriers had run away, and we had nothing to draw the water up with, so the men were all distracted. Some of them let their caps down to draw it up. Being all satisfied, we proceeded on our march, and put a man from each company in charge of the cooks, for fear they should desert.

The country all round is a wild jungle, or wood, low and bushy, which made it very bad for us to wind our way through it, and the air close. We came to another well at four o'clock, when all was as before. We pitched our camp a little before seven o'clock in the morning. We got our breakfast in good time.

On Thursday we struck camp at half-past twelve o'clock a.m. We then procured plenty of water; it was carried upon bullocks, in leather bags, one hanging upon each side. The country all round is jungle, with here and there a few large trees scattered. We pitched camp at six o'clock. It is surprising to see what a difference plenty of water makes. We ate nothing to support us, but drank gallons of water. Our men began to look pale and bad; the eyes sank into the head. We looked wild and ghastly, and we were as thin as shadows.

On Friday we struck camp at ten o'clock. The men marched off pretty well this morning, but soon began to be as bad as ever. They commenced falling out by numbers. We pressed more carriages to bring our sick into camp. Some of the men were taken with fever. One man was carried into camp by some women. He had fallen to the rear, and lay down in the bush and died. We buried him in the sand, as he fell, in a desert wild all around: we had no useless coffin to put him in, and long before morning would he be food for the wild beast. God rest his soul! The officer of his company read the funeral service over him.

We pitched camp at five o'clock. Some of our bullock-drivers deserted with their bullocks, when their carts were burnt. They were very fine, being so beautifully carved, and brass and steel let into the wood.

The men had not gone far; as soon as they saw their "accrys" on fire, they came back begging and crying; but it was of no use, and they were well beaten too. They jumped about and cried—wrang their hands—and supplicated; but all was useless—their carriages were committed to the flames.

On Saturday we struck camp at half-past 12 o'clock. We marched over a very large, sandy plain; the sand being so very light, it made it very bad marching. It rose in clouds, and as there was no wind to carry it away, I really thought we should all have been stifled together. We were nearly blinded, and our nostrils were completely choked up; so we were obliged to open our mouths to get breath, which caused them to become full and dry and parched up. Alas! who could describe the scene—men fell faint and exhausted in the ranks? One man fell dead. He was relieved from this world of trouble, and many more wished for the same fate. We scraped a hole in the sand, and there laid him.

We pressed more water-carriers, and put them with the guard, so that they could not desert so easily; but they gave us the slip everywhere they could. I do not wonder at them, for they had to work like horses.

Our commissariat began serving out bad grog; but it was reported to the colonel, and he made him glad to give good; for

F

this was about all we had to support us. Of food we ate little
or none: it might be said that water was our only support.
We appeared as if we were never satisfied. We did not drink
less than four or five gallons per day. As soon as we had
drunk a good draught, it would come pouring through our skin.
Our clothes were soon soaked through, and we had not a dry
thread upon us. In a very short time, if it had not come
through the skin, we should have been dead.

The colonel received intelligence that our rear would be
attacked, but no enemy made his appearance. Most of the
villages were deserted as we marched by them, for fear their
inhabitants should be pressed. We pitched camp at 5 o'clock.
On Sunday we struck camp at half-past 12 o'clock. We were
better off for water that day. We crossed a large plain, but the
sand was firmer, and we got on pretty well; though a number of men
fell out through weakness. About two o'clock we came on the
borders of the plain of Alliwal, where the battle was fought
against the Sikhs in 1846. We left the battle-ground about
two miles to our left, passed a small fort that closed its gates
upon our troops at that time, and pitched camp at 4 o'clock.

We struck camp at 11 o'clock. We made two marches this
day, being the Sabbath, instead of resting.

This was a very long day's march, over sandy deserts
and plains. The water being short the horrors became
past describing. We drew near to a well some time in the
morning, and the confusion all round was fearful,—the men
rushing and pushing to get at it, some letting their caps fall into
it, and some their bayonets; and I quite expected some of the
men would go in. One poor fellow, in endeavouring to get up,
had fallen, and was begging most pitifully that some one would give
him a draught to save his life; but, God help him! he spent
his breath in vain. The doctor seeing him in this deplorable
state, asked a man to give him a drink, but was refused.
Every one must take care of himself: all respect for one another

was gone. I was very nearly done up myself. Here my tongue was swollen, and mouth parched up; and I felt very weak. My brain seemed to be on fire, and my eyes as if they would jump out of my head. I felt as if I was done; but I made a rush at the water and got some. God knows what a relief I felt, as if I had lost a great load ! When most of the throng was over, I filled a tin flask which I carried with me for that purpose; so did all others who had them. Our officers were as bad as the men. What thousands there are in England who do not know the value of a drop of water !

Towards the end of the march the wind rose, and drove the sand in such clouds that it cut our faces, and drove in heaps like snow. We pitched camp at 5 o'clock on Monday morning the 21st.

We struck camp at 12 o'clock p.m. To give a proper description of this day, is more than I can do. The wind blew a perfect hurricane, and the sand rose in clouds, cutting our faces and eyes dreadfully, and completely darkening the air. The country all round was a barren desert.

Officers and men became frantic for want of water, and our guides informed us that we must go six miles further before we could get any more; those who had flasks filled them. Mine did not hold more than half-a-pint. I could have sold it for any money before we got far on the way. The wind blew fearfully, and the sand rose in clouds; so that we could not see one another. My company was on the advance guard, and we lost the regiment on the plains. The sand rose in such clouds that we could not see them, and the wind blew so strong that they could not hear our bugle sound "the close." Our officers rode in all directions in search of them; at length, they succeeded. The storm abated for a short time, but soon commenced again, and the sand rose in such clouds, and the wind was so hot, that the men fell by numbers. The want of water was past everything—the best and strongest men were beaten up

—the cry of " water, water," " well, well," was heard on every side. Men were in the greatest agonies. I found my drop of water of more value than gold ; but how I stood it more than the rest I do not know. I carried a bit of ginger in my mouth always —perhaps it was that. Although I was ill, very ill, and wished I was dead, yet God was good and merciful to me, and I pulled through.

We came to a well and a few Indian huts at 4 o'clock. All became disorder ; men rushed out of the ranks like madmen, and all the officers could do to keep order was useless. I and two others got into the huts, and the natives gave us all the water they had ; so we did pretty well. We halted here about three quarters of an hour, when the wind dropped to a calm. We saw a large, black, dismal-looking cloud rising to our right—for it was now daylight. In a short time after, a gentle breeze sprang up, and ruffled the sand as it came slowly along. We all expected it was going to rain ; but alas ! alas ! we were mistaken,—the breeze began to be stronger and of a cool kind, which made us shudder—though not a cold shudder ; something seemed to be awful about it.

The wind now got to the east, and began to blow stronger ; and the men fell sick by numbers. I felt very bad. It was a sickly kind of a feel. There the men lay, groaning in the greatest of agony. The doctors and apothecaries were all bustle, bleeding the men as they lay upon the sand, until pools of black blood were spread all over the ground. It was a most shocking sight to behold. There they were,—some dead, and some dying. The dead were as follows :—one captain, one sergeant, and four privates. One man shot himself, to put an end to his troubles ; thus making a total of seven dead, and very near half the regiment sick. Luckily, the wind changed to the south-west, and the sickness abated. Those who were not so very bad revived all at once.

Our poor colonel was nearly distracted, not knowing what

to do for the best. The wind by this time was blowing as bad
as it did when we first started, and the sand rose in masses.
One part of the regiment lost the other in the storm; but the
officers rode all round, and the bugles sounding "the close,"
we got together again.

We pitched our camp about six o'clock, with those tents at
least which had arrived; for some of the tents and baggage did
not come until late in the day; they got lost in the sand-
storm. Two of our camp followers had fallen dead. Our
colonel went all over the ground to see that his men were as
comfortable as they could be. The wind dropped in the
evening. We paraded at six o'clock, to bury our dead; they
were sown up in their beds, and put altogether into a pit which
was made for that purpose. The captain was put in a few
boards, knocked up together, and buried by their side. We
fired three volleys of blank cartridge over them. The colonel
read the funeral service. The only thing that marked the spot
was a few trees near an Indian village.

During the time we were burying them, a thunderstorm rose.
The sky was one complete sheet of fire, and the peals of thunder were dreadful, as if the heavens were coming down. The
whole of the men looked pale, sad, and downcast. The doctor
told the colonel that he must halt the next day, as it was
impossible to move the whole of the sick. One man went out
of his mind, and ran through the jungle, and was not captured
until a few days after.

We halted on the 23rd—a very fine, bright day, though the
sun was very hot. We struck camp at ten o'clock. A shower
of rain fell just as we had packed up; and it came so very
heavily that it fairly took our breath: we were completely
soaked through, although it did not last more than a quarter of
an hour. We did not mind being wet, for the rain laid the
sand and made the marching better. This was the first time
we had marched in anything like comfort, and it was a very

long day's march. At about three o'clock we passed the village of Boosean, noted as the first place that the enemy's scouts were seen in, in 1846, when the Sikhs invaded the British territories. We pitched camp at five o'clock; our tents arrived about seven. I mounted guard here for the first time as corporal.

We pitched our camp upon the battle-field of Moodkee, and in front of the village from which the battle took its name. It is a small place, built of mud, and surrounded by a mud wall. The field all around is thickly scattered with bushes and sand-hills. About two hundred yards to the front of our camp stood two large banyan trees, which marked the spot where General Sale and General McGaskill (who fell at the battle) were buried; and a few hundred yards at the back of the camp, by the side of a group of small trees and bushes, was a mound of earth, beneath which lay many a brave man who fell in fighting the battle for "Old England," in December 1845. Little more more than two years ago, the field all around was strewn with human bones and skulls. This was the first battle fought by the British and Sikh armies. It took place after our troops had been marching all day, the Sikh army making the attack.

A fearful storm commenced about nine o'clock, p.m. The sand rose in such clouds as I had never before seen. The thunder and lightning were frightful—beyond description. All was in total darkness, and the wind blew several of our tents down, and the soldiers off their legs, so that we were obliged to lie down and let the sand drift over us. One of our sentinels was carried away from his post, and could not find it again until the storm abated, which it did about eleven o'clock.

On Thursday, the 24th, we struck camp at twelve o'clock, p.m. We were very well off for water, and got on very well. The country all round was jungle, and, as daylight broke, we saw the bones of men, horses, and beasts which were killed.

We pitched camp at five o'clock, upon the plains of Feroze-
shah, famous for the Sikh entrenched camp, and the battle
fought there in January, 1846. One camel-load of baggage
was taken here—we supposed by some of the villagers.

I visited the village. We pitched camp upon the very ground
where the British army took up its position, previous to the battle.
The village is just in front. It was strongly occupied by the
enemy's infantry, with several mines round it. The well that
we had to get our water from had several skeletons in it; but
we had to make use of it. The plain is very open and cultivated, and many thousand human bones there lie bleaching in
the sun, as they have been ploughed up to the top of the earth.
This battle, too, is remarkable as one where the 62nd regiment
was panic-struck, or (as is reported) ran away. They got
very much cut up. A beautiful monument is erected here to
the memory of a gallant officer who fell in this battle.

At twelve o'clock on the morning of the 25th, we marched
on very comfortably, it being the last day, and we got plenty of
water. As daylight broke, we saw nothing but a large sandy
plain in front of us—not a tree nor shrub to be seen. After
marching for about an hour we could see in front, at a very
long distance, the station of Ferozepoor—the place we were to
halt at until further orders. We did not like the looks of it
as we drew near; it appeared a barren, desert place. Still, we
were glad to halt for a short time, to rest; for we were about
overcome.

We arrived at the barracks a little after five o'clock on the
morning of the 26th (Saturday). The barrack is built very
slightly, of sunburnt brick. It had not been up more than four
years. To the east stands the fort; it is a large place—but all
of mud or sun-burnt brick. It was the depôt for stores and
ammunition, and all kinds of war equipage: such as guns,
powder, shot, shell, tentage, muskets, ammunition, wagons, gun
carriages, clothing, and provision.

The town of Ferozepoor is about four miles from the barracks —rather better than half way to the river Sutlej. It is but a small place, though there are a few good brick buildings of the native kind. It appeared to be an old town. They seemed to manufacture cloth in it; but all around was a wild and a wilderness-looking country.

We were very crowded in the rooms; some of the men were obliged to lie upon the floor, and the barracks were very dirty. We had not been here long before a great deal of sickness began, and we lost a large number of men. They died very suddenly —mostly of fever and apoplexy, the climate being so very hot, and the men drinking very hard of grog. We had very good water there. Every thing was very dear: we could not get any kind of vegetables, so we ate rice instead. I never was well all the time we lay there; it was a very dreadful place for storms— the sand came in such clouds that we had darkness all day. The sand drifts blew in heaps and rucks like snow. I suppose the cause is that the country is a desert all round. Sometimes will be seen numbers of whirlwinds, twisting the sand up as they go.

We received orders to be in readiness to march, and to take the field at a moment's notice. The General inspected us, and gave us great credit for our marching in the hot season, and for the general good conduct of the regiment. One wing of the 14th regiment of Light Dragoons was lying here with us. The men looked very bad, like us, and buried a great number of men. There were four regiments of native infantry, and two of cavalry, with European and native artillery. We received news of several engagements having been fought by the native and Sikh troops. A great many conspiracies, and a deal of bribery occurred at Lahore. Several of our native soldiers had been hung, and the church had been undermined, and powder put under to blow the men up whilst in it; but the design was found out—in fact, there was a great deal of treachery going on. The people here were very saucy.

CHAPTER V.

WE lay at this station until the middle of July, and had buried
a great many of our comrades: scarcely a day passed but we
put some poor man into the grave; and we looked more
like moving ghosts than men about to face a foe. Men were
fairly driven to distraction through torture. We were the
most troubled with "the prickly heat."

This is owing to the warmth of the weather and the blood.
The body breaks out all over with small red pimples, with
water in them; and they itch unbearably—or rather, more like
pins and needles pricking us all over. Some have their bodies
covered all over, so that it would be impossible to lay a six-
pence on a place free from the pimples. Then the flies and
musquitoes are in many millions, and insects by night in many
thousands; altogether, we never had any comfort. Many men
betook themselves to the canteen, and there drank until they
could not stand. Some of them would take as much as a
quart of grog at a night, and would be carried insensible either
to the guard-room or to their barracks, and be found dead on
their beds the next morning, suffocated in liquor, or removed
in a fit of apoplexy, brought on by the drink and the heat of
the weather. Some lay upon their cots, cursing and swearing,
wishing that the ship had sunk that brought them to India; or
that they were dead; when, at last, they would be driven
to despair, and either blow out their brains, or jump into a
well, thus putting an end to their existence.

In general orders which we received, we and all the troops
at this station were appointed to be the second brigade of the

G

first division of the army of the Punjaub, under the command of
Major General Whish, C.B.; our first colonel to be brigadier of
the second brigade, and Lieutenant-Colonel Harvey to be brigadier of the first brigade, composed of the following regiments :
—first brigade; H.M. 10th regt. native, 8th regt. N.I., and
52nd regt., with one troop of native artillery, two squadrons of
the 11th native cavalry, and two squadrons of irregular native
cavalry of the 14th regt. (then lying at Lahore). Second
brigade : H.M. 32nd regt., and 49th, 51st, and 72nd regts. of
N. I., with two squadrons of the 11th native cavalry, two squadrons of the 14th irregular cavalry, one of the 10th N. I. C., and
one troop of native artillery (lying at Ferozepoor). We were to
be ready to take the field at a moment's notice, to march to
Mooltan, the seat of war.

On the 18th of July, shot and shell began to arrive by hundreds of camel-loads every day, and warlike stores of every
description. On the 19th the artillery park moved to the river
Sutlej, a distance of about eight miles ; the artillerymen being
employed in loading the boats.

On the 21st several artillerymen died from over-exertion and
the heat of the weather. The native troops marched in the
morning on the road leading to Baalpoor, under the command
of brigadier Markham, and in charge of the siege-train.

A guard of my regiment marched out on the morning of the
31st, at three o'clock, to the river Sutlej, to escort the ammunition and war stores down the river to Baalpoor, where they
marched for Mooltan. They were 150 strong. They lost two
men in the river; they were bathing and got on the quicksand,
which took them away; so they sank to rise no more. All
kinds of reports were now flying about respecting the enemy.

On Thursday, August 10th, we received the long-expected
route to march for Mooltan. The men welcomed the news
with a loud hurra! All hands seemed in good spirits, and
ready to meet the enemy at any time or place. We got our

tents and baggage all ready by the evening, and the sick and weakly men were to be left at Ferozepoor; but all such as were likely to get better in a short time, were taken to the river to the boats, in order to go with us. All was bustle during the night. I was very sick, and had been so for some time. I felt very faint and weak, and not much fit either for a long march or to face an enemy; but sooner than have it said that I shrunk from meeting one, I made up my mind to die upon the way. Three or four men acted completely the coward; they made themselves sick purposely. The men plagued them, and always after led them a life like a dog's.

On Friday, the 11th, at ten o'clock, we paraded. We were composed of six companies and head quarters, leaving one company to take charge of the station, until the 29th regiment should arrive, to be on the reserve. We marched out about 750 strong, our band playing, "The girl I left behind me," and "Should auld acquaintance be forgot." We had been waiting for half an hour for our colonel coming; but who could murmur, when all knew the feelings of a husband taking the last farewell of his wife—the dearest of all on earth to him? How little did he think it would be the last kiss he would ever take from those lips. They were both in years, upwards of sixty; and had lived happily together for half that time. They had no children.

The morning was very sultry and close, and as we passed through the market, the sand rose thickly. The men being so weak, it was as much as they could do to bear it. When our colonel joined us, it was very dark, and we could not see him plainly, but could tell by his voice that he was troubled in mind, though not with fear; for a braver soldier never drew a sword. His name was Potton, Lieut. Colonel commanding the 32nd regiment.

We had got on only a very short distance, when men began to fall out through weakness. Several were so bad that they

were taken back to the station, and before we had got four
miles on the way, I was obliged to fall to the rear through
weakness. All the carriages were already full, as upwards of
one hundred had already fallen out; and as I came gently
along, I passed numbers more lying on the ground. One poor
fellow I observed was in a dreadful state. He called out,
"Who's there? why the d—— do you not blow out my brains
and put me out of my trouble?" and then in a short time he
began to pray for water. I still kept getting on the road, and
passed numbers more lying upon the ground. Two men died.
I met the elephants coming back to pick up the sick.

We arrived at the river before daylight, and got our baggage
on board as soon as possible—by 12 o'clock; and then we were
told off to the boats. Some of them took 30 men, and some
but 16. We were very crowded and uncomfortable. We had
not room to lie down. We were together like so many
pigs. This was on account of our being ordered off before any
more had arrived. They are very rudely constructed boats.
They have flat bottoms, and will float in six inches of water.
The planks are pegged together, and the nicks plugged up with
cotton, or old rags; but the water is continually oozing through,
one of the natives being nearly employed in baling it out. The
top and sides were covered with reeds, to keep off the sun. A
large oar is fixed on either side, which three or four men pull
at. We got all the sick and everything on board, and started
at four o'clock. We did not go far that evening; we halted
at sunset, and all hands set to and cooked. We moored the
boats by the bankside during the night. We buried the two
men who died on the bank. We did not sleep in the boats,
but took our beds and spread them upon the ground, and there
reposed for the night, whilst the jackalls and other animals
were howling round us by hundreds.

On the 12th, we drew our rations at daylight, and cooked
them. Some of our men were bathing in the river, when one

got upon the sand and was drowned; and another man was very near meeting the same fate, but was saved by one of the natives. Our bugles sounded the advance, and we put off at sunrise. We sailed until sunset, when we halted for the night, and bivouacked upon the ground, as on the preceding night. The river at this season of the year is very high; this is through the sun melting the snow upon the Himalaya mountains; so that the rivers in this country are always the highest in the hot season. The river varies in breadth from a quarter of a mile to a mile. The banks are very low, and the bed of the river often changes. At one season the current washes away one side, and another season the other. It is very rapid. We went from 20 to 30 miles per day, and some days more. The country on either side was well cultivated, and numbers of villages were studded about the banks. We saw several alligators upon the sand, basking in the sun; and large flocks of birds of all kinds were to be seen, such as geese, ducks, pelicans, and many more, which I have forgotten. There are numbers of vultures. We continued our course down the river, every day being nearly the same, up to the 16th.

On that day we caught a number of hares; they were very tame—we knocked them over with a stick. We also caught a cat-fish; the head of these fish is much like that of a cat, having a whisker, and when caught they cry like a hare or rabbit. We passed a small fort on the right hand side of the river: there was a great deal of jungle on both sides, and all looked very wild and dismal. A number of snakes were seen about. I saw several in the river; they followed the boats, and appeared as if they intended to come into them. They skipped along the top of the water with their heads up; and I do believe they would have attacked us if we had not killed them.

On the 18th, we halted at sunset, as usual, and most of us were walking out into the woods—some getting wood for cooking, others looking for hares—when we heard a gurry strike seven o'clock. We started; for we knew that we were in the enemy's territories. We climbed up trees to look out for them. We could see some tents about a mile away. We came back, and by this time an order reached us that it was the 72nd regiment of native infantry encamped, waiting for our arrival, in order to march to Mooltan with us, with two squadrons of native cavalry. The cause of these troops being here was, that we should not march in such small bodies, in case the enemy might attack us before we made a junction with the army at Mooltan. Our orders were that we were to disembark, and get our baggage loaded upon the cattle immediately, and be ready for marching at one o'clock.

That hour on the day following soon arrived, and we started off from the river. We wound our way through the jungle, which is very thick and bad for marching. I was very weak, and felt very unwell. We did not march far that morning, pitching camp before daylight, upon a very rugged sandy place, near to a village, which was deserted by all the natives, except a few old people. I supposed they had gone to join in the war against us; the old people looked very surly at us.

On Sunday the 20th, we struck camp at one o'clock. The night was very close. Four men and I were left to clear camp ground, and see all the baggage up. I got worse, and it was as much as I could do to keep up; and I never should have done, had I not swallowed five drams of grog, about a pint in a bottle. I found that I was likely to give in; so I drank the whole of my grog at once—kill or cure. This of course put a false spirit in me; however, I reached the camp. We marched a long way that day, and numbers fell upon the way. One man fell dead. The country all round was in a most deplorable state, the villages being deserted. I arrived at camp about nine o'clock, in charge of the four men. The day turned out dreadfully hot: we lay in the tents panting for breath. I still

got worse, and about five o'clock in the evening I reported
myself sick, and went to hospital. A most awful sight here
presented itself; all the sick tents were full, so that they were
obliged to get more from the company's tents. Dozens of men
lay in the agonies of pain, whilst others were struggling for the
last breath of life. I thought what a horrible sight it was; and
I lay upon the ground thinking upon my own fate, for I felt
very bad. I could not tell how long I should be before I was
food for some wild beast. I began to get very low-spirited
and given to fret; when, all at once, I thought that would not
do: so I rallied my feelings and walked about, and began to
think I should soon be better. This and the medicine the
doctor had administered soon began to revive me, and I felt a
great deal better. I knew that numbers of men made themselves worse by giving way to their feelings, for the doctors
would always tell the men to keep up their spirits. Our officers
came round to visit the sick, and were very kind to us; but we
were the worst off for carriages to carry the sick, and we could
could not leave them behind. The heat was above 100 degrees,
and the water was very bad, on account of the wells not being
used, which caused the water to be stagnant and black, and
smell very offensively, so that we were obliged to stop our
noses whilst we drank.

On the 21st our doctor told us that all, who could possibly
march, must; for carriages could not be got. I for one volun-
teered, as I thought I was a great deal better; and we were not
to carry our arms or accoutrements, but to go at our ease, and
march in front of the column, to be out of the cloud of sand
that would rise.

The morning was hotter and closer than ever I felt it before,
and the wind was awful—fairly parching our flesh. We had
not marched more than two miles upon the road before men
began to fall dead in the ranks, and numbers fell senseless to
the ground. Our line of march was strewed with dead, dying,

and sick. The moanings and cries were heartrending. Our doctors and apothecaries were all engaged in bleeding; but as the night was very dark, they could not find the vein, and they cut gashes across the arm any way, so as to get blood. Some would bleed and some would not, for the blood was congealed in the veins, and as black as jet. All our carriages were crowded, and even the baggage cattle were obliged to carry some of the sick. The cry for water was past all describing; the mouth and tongue were swollen and parched, the eyes looked wild and ghastly, and ready to start out of the head. How little do the people of England know the hardships of a poor soldier in India! Such soldiers as the guards, and many other regiments, do not know what a soldier's life is; nor ever were under the fire of an enemy, or smelt powder in their lives. Still they get just as well paid and thought of as we were.

As we went along nothing but horrible sights met the eye. Men lay upon the sand by dozens, gasping for breath; some would try to utter some one's name—perhaps a dear old parent's, a gray-headed old father's, or a heart-broken lonely old mother's, or it might be a lovely wife's, left to lament the loss of a soldier husband. But, alas! the brain was burning, and the mind wandering; the sufferers' strength was going and death stared them in the face. What could be done? All the skill of a physician could not restore them. I saw our old colonel looking at them, and he exclaimed, "Oh, my poor men, my fine regiment—what shall I do?" I felt very sorry for him; for he was in great trouble. There was no friendly neighbour's house to leave them at, or kind friend who would be glad to lend a helping hand: no, far different there—we were in an enemy's country!

We pitched our camp at sunrise. The day was hotter than the oldest native could remember. We could not bear ourselves. Our beasthes were employed in bringing water, and dashing it over us as we lay upon the ground, to keep the fever down. As one man died he was carried out, and another came in his place. They were well and dead in an hour. They would turn black about the eyes and the finger nails, and froth at the mouth. One of my companions came into the tent, when I asked him to sit down, but he said he was not going to stop, as he felt better; but, thought I, "you never will," (for his eyes, lips, and finger nails were black) and he was no more in less than a quarter of an hour. The number of men who fell sick in the day was 175, and 14 dead. The heat in the tents was 130 degrees. All our dead were buried in a hole together, at sunset; and long before morning the wild beasts had torn them up and dragged them to pieces. I would have given the world to have been in England at this time, yet I thought it would never do to yield to my feelings and these sights; for such is the life of a soldier; and, as I expected, I had got many such to face.

Another day or two like the last followed. On the evening of the 23rd, we expected an attack from the enemy to be made upon our camp at night; so we received orders to lie upon our arms, and be upon the alert. Two companies were ready accoutred, waiting for the attack, but none was made.

As we marched along on the two following days, I noticed that the country all round had been well cultivated, but the crops had been neglected, and were withering for want of water.

We made a junction with the army at Mooltan on the morning of the 25th of August, at about seven o'clock. A number of officers came to meet us: also, our brigadier and General Whish. Our brigadier had arrived with the native troops a few days before. The first brigade reached Mooltan three or four days before from Lahore. The enemy attacked them on the way, but was steadily repulsed, leaving a number of dead on the field. The loss on our side was two killed and several wounded.

H

We took up our position on the left of the first division, with the artillery park in the centre, and about three miles in front of Mooltan. It had a grand appearance, and was surrounded by beautiful topes of trees, especially the date and cocoa-nut. There were two large churches, having a fine appearance, towering far above the rest of the buildings; but they were doomed to destruction—noble and grand as they were. We could see the guns upon the walls by looking through a telescope.

The morning of the 26th was very clear after the rain, and it was surprising to see what a number of men recovered. Fifteen or twenty of them went out of the sick list, and I felt to be getting quite strong; but I met with another adventure which was nearly putting me out of the world.

It was about nine o'clock in the morning when a native came round the camp to sell milk; and, as we thought he was one of our camp followers, we took no further notice of him, eagerly buying his milk. In my tent there were twelve men, of whom ten bought some, and several others in other tents, I being one of the number. We had not drunk it more than half an hour, before we began to froth at the mouth, and swell and vomit. The tale was soon told—poison was in the milk! The doctors were soon with us, and by applying proper remedies in time, we all recovered; but as I was the weakest, I was the worst. I never suffered such pain in my life before; I felt in my mind it would be better for me to die, and be out of my troubles at once. However, the next morning I recovered.

On the 27th we changed camp at five o'clock, a.m. The whole army took up a fresh position, about a mile nearer to the town, and a little to the left of it. We could see the enemy upon the move. They watched us very closely, but made no attack. Lieut. Edwardes (in command of our native allied troops) was encamped about a mile to our left. Sharp skirmishes took place during the night; but we did not exchange a shot. Our outlying picquets and the enemy's were not more than a musket-shot from each other.

The firing of our native troops was kept up briskly all night on the 28th, with musketry and cannon; but the enemy did not seem inclined to make any advance upon us. Our men became better in health, and the hospital was nearly empty. Some of them went out before they were strong; for they were afraid there would be an engagement whilst they were on the sick report, and it should be said they were sickening, and skulking, and acting cowardly. All were in good spirits, and wanted to have a contest, to try their courage and their maiden steel.

CHAPTER VI.

THE siege-train arrived before Mooltan from Baalpoor, on Monday, Sep. 4th, 1848, with the 150 men of my regiment, who left on the 31st of July, in charge of the train at Ferozepoor. The company we left there joined us the day before—this completed the whole of our regiment. We were now about one thousand strong. Shot, and shell, and ammunition, and other things for the siege, had been arriving for the three previous days by hundreds of camel-loads. Everything appeared now about ready for the commencement. The firing had been going on every day, on both sides, at long distance. I was upon the outlying picquet one night, when I was bitten by a scorpion on the bottom of the leg, which swelled, and was greatly inflamed and very painful for about a fortnight, when the piece of flesh affected dropped out and the leg got well.

On the morning of the 5th, the whole army assembled at sunrise, and formed line in front of the city, for the purpose of sending in a proclamation, when a royal salute of twenty-one guns was fired. The enemy answered it by firing three shots from their guns upon the walls. The shots fell about two or three hundred yards in front of us, but did us no harm. This of course told us that they intended to fight. We could see their scouts upon the alert. The proclamation was as follows:

"By Major-General W. S. Whish, C.B., commanding the army before Mooltan, to the inhabitants and garrison thereof.

"I invite both to an unconditional surrender, within twenty-four hours after the firing of a royal salute at sunrise to-morrow, the 5th of September, in honour of Her Majesty, the Queen of Great Britain, and her ally Maharajah Dhuleep S ng.

"I shall otherwise, in obedience to the orders of the supreme Government of India, commence hostilities on a scale that must ensure early destruction to the rebel traitor and his adherents, who, having begun that resistance to lawful authority with a most cowardly act of treachery and murder, seek to uphold their unrighteous cause by an appeal to arms, which every one must know to be hypocrisy.

"If the town be surrendered to me, as above suggested, private property will be respected, and the garrison of the fort will be permitted to withdraw unmolested, on giving up Dewan Moolraj and his immediate associates, and laying down their arms at one of the eastern gates of the town and fort respectively.

"Given under my hand, this 4th day of Sep. 1848,

"(Signed,) W. S. WHISH, C.B.,

"Major General, commanding the Mooltan Field Force."

On the 6th, we removed camp, taking up a fresh position to our left and front nearer to the city. This position we intended to keep whilst the siege went on.

As the weather was so warm, the 72nd regiment of native infantry was taken out for the purpose of driving in one of the enemy's outposts. This was necessary, as it was so near our camp. It was done in good style, with trifling loss. We had sharp firing all night. They did not like losing their post. One or two of our camp followers were taken prisoners, by going too far to the front.

From the 7th the siege commenced. The first ground was broken, and active hostilities were begun by the British troops; and as I calculated things up in my own mind, perhaps it would not be amiss to state them before the description of the siege commences.

We had not more than eight thousand men of all arms and ranks, and about thirty-two pieces of ordnance of all sizes; and out of these there were twelve field pieces (six pounders), and the largest battering guns were thirty-two pounders. Out of this force only two thousand were Europeans, all the rest being natives. It is true that our allied troops, under the command of Lieut. Edwardes, amounted to eight thousand more; but we might as well have been without them, as they were not to be depended upon; nor could they fight with us, being undisciplined troops. They were dressed the same as the enemy, and were of the same country : therefore we were as liable to fire into them as into the enemy.

Mooltan is a large city, with strong walls all round, and many strong outposts (well occupied by resolute men), besides numbers of entrenchments and redoubts ; and it appeared to be well supplied with artillery. The fort (close to the city) is one of the strongest in the country, and commands all round it; and it was reported that upwards of thirty thousand men occupied the garrison. At this rate, before the siege began, I thought we were no more able to take the place than fly.

At one o'clock, p.m., a party of native troops (about seven hundred), and a party of sappers, were ordered to the front, to begin entrenching. They commenced the work under a sharp fire from the enemy, but at long distance ; so they received no damage. At sunset, four hundred and fifty of my regiment, and three hundred and fifty of the 10th regiment were ordered to the front, to relieve the natives. As the weather was so hot, we went in our shirts, with our accoutrements upon us, and a peck and shovel upon our shoulders. We arrived at the place appointed at dusk, and immediately commenced our works. The enemy did not fire upon us for some time ; they appeared as if they were watching our movements ; or rather listening, for it was dark. We had a covering party of our allied troops, with two field guns.

We had been working about an hour, when a shot came whizzing among us, and struck the ground about ten yards from me. This was the first shot I ever was near, or heard. It made me feel fluttered for a short time; but it was not many minutes before a shower of balls came singing over us, and then a cannon-shot came, falling short, followed by a number more, though all were harmless. The enemy tried to make an advance, but met a sharp fire from our covering party, which kept them in check. This was a good place to put a lazy man in; for the harder he worked the more he got shelter from the shot. Our hands were very painful; large blood blisters rose, and the blood trickled down our fingers. This need not be wondered at, for we were not used to handling tools. We soon got a place deep, sufficient to cover us, and then made it wider after. As we had to work with our accoutrements upon us, and our muskets by our sides, it reminded me of a passage of scripture, where it says they worked at the building of the walls of Jerusalem with one hand, holding the sword in the other. We were relieved by the sepoys before daybreak; they took post all day, and kept the outposts and enemy in check.

On the 8th the enemy made several attempts to regain their post, but were repulsed. Our sepoys lost a man or two. We relieved them at night, and began to erect a battery for four long eighteen pounders, and we ran another battery to the right. We got the guns into play, which did fine execution. The enemy appeared to be getting vexed, for they opened a heavy fire of musketry or cannon upon us. They might as well, however, have kept them at home; for as we never returned a shot, they could not tell whereabouts we were, as it was so dark. They then got very bold; they came so near that we could hear them talking. They tried all they could do to draw our fire out, but all was useless, as we kept our fire reserved. We were relieved by the sepoys in the morning, after a hard night's work.

The firing on both sides was sharp on the 9th; there was heavy cannonading, with terrible volleys of musketry. It was considered right to make the sepoys do a little more work, as there were five regiments of them, and two only of us; and the weather being so hot, they were the best able to bear it. At dusk, in the evening, the right wing of the 10th regiment, and a strong party of sepoys, went to the trenches, in order to relieve the day party. Before they had been there long, the enemy became so daring, that it was thought it would be prudent to make them keep at a distance; and two villages in front, being strongly occupied by the enemy, with walls and entrenchments all round them, which were a great annoyance to us, as the enemy sheltered in them, and we wanted to run our works up towards them (our colonel having charge of the whole of the advance works for the night), it was agreed that an attack should be made upon the villages. It was, however, foolish to attempt the assault in the night, upon villages which we were not the least acquainted with.

At nine o'clock, p.m., when the attack was made, it was very dark. I was in camp, for we had no part in it. The trees and villages appeared in a complete blaze of fire. The roll of musketry and roar of cannon was terrible, for about an hour; when it slackened, and ended in our troops being repulsed, with the loss of two of the 10th regiment, and one of the 72nd regiment of native infantry taken prisoners. The killed were two men of the 10th, with one officer and seven men and sepoys. Our colonel had his horse shot under him, and a ball passed through his cap, close by his temples. This showed that our troops were defeated in the attempt. The enemy fought very desperately. Our men could not see where they were going, so were obliged to retire. The enemy were determined to annoy us as much as they could: they commenced sending balls into our camp from the guns upon the walls. They came tearing through the air, and fell into our camp amongst the tents; but, strange as it may appear, not a man was hurt by them. A horse was killed at the back of the camp. The ball passed through his body; and on another occasion a ball went through one of the sepoy's tents, striking the pot which they were cooking with upon the fire, and sending other articles flying about.

We had pitched our camp too near the city. We went to relieve the working party at midnight, and commenced erecting a battery for four large guns to play upon the villages on which the attack was made. Day broke upon us before we had got the guns into battery; the enemy soon saw the advantage, and quickly made use of it. They brought every gun they could to bear upon us. The balls flew like hail, and tore and ploughed up the ground all around us, whilst we were working with all our might to get the guns into play, which we did soon. One of our artillery horses was killed. Their infantry came so close, that we were obliged to give them a few rounds of grape and canister, which did good execution, and made them take shelter in their intrenchments.

As day broke, we had a good view of the two villages. The further one was the largest, and had a large temple in it; and about half a mile in the rear of it was a great sand-mound, with a battery of guns upon it, which they played upon us. They were also surrounded with large trees and some low brush wood.

At about eight o'clock the enemy became so daring that we expected an attack. Heavy firing took place between us for about an hour. We gave it them warmly, but they were no-wise daunted. They returned it sharply. Our loss was one brigadier, and several sepoys wounded. I felt the wind of several balls as they whizzed by me, and others struck the ground and drove the earth into my face. I saw several very narrow escapes. I was quite deaf with the roar of cannon, which was continually playing over my head. My ears were

I

very painful. I thought the blood would gush out. Our men
were anxious to get at the enemy, and asked the officers to let
them have a "go" at them. I saw our colonel in the morning:
he looked very pale, and in great trouble of mind. He did
not like being defeated: but he was in good spirits, and joked
with the men. He called us his green linnets. We asked him
to let us have an attack upon the villages. He told us that
we should have our will in a short time. We were relieved by
two companies of my regiment, and two of the 10th, and some
sepoys, at ten o'clock in the morning. One of the 10th regiment
lay upon a bank about half way between our post and the
enemy. He appeared to be dead: he fell on the night of the
9th, at the attack upon the villages, and could not be brought
in. We dared not go to fetch him, although several attempts
were made to do so, as the enemy directed such a fire upon us;
and they dare not go to cut him up, as we directed such a fire
upon them; so this was a sort of neutral ground between us.
Our men began to be very impatient; they wanted to be trying
their hand at cold steel. Our colonel told us to have patience,
and we should try our hands ere long. We told him we were
ready and willing to follow him wherever he might lead us.

On Sunday (the 10th), when we arrived at camp in the morning, one of our men found an unwelcome bedfellow in his bed,
in the shape of one of the enemy's cannon balls. A nine-pounder
had struck the ground outside our tent, and came through the
tent-wall, and lodged in his bed.

The enemy pressed our sepoys so close at the intrenchments
that two companies of my regiment were sent down to reinforce
them. There was sharp firing all day. The enemy still kept
sending us a few iron messengers amongst our tents. We had
no rest again on that day. The men were all getting weary
and fatigued. We had had no rest from the commencement,
and but little to eat. It was quite laughable to see our camp-
followers running to hide themselves when they heard the whizz

ing of the balls coming. They would squat down behind the
tent walls, or any where. They were so frightened they did not
know where to go. I told some of them not to be afraid. They
would say, in their language, "If a ball strikes me, and I am
killed, you would say, 'oh, never mind—it's only a black man.'"
A shot passed through one of the tents of the 51st regiment
of native infantry; but it hurt no one. Several men had been
wounded at the advanced works, and it was very hot for the
two companies in charge of the works. The sun had been
sufficient to roast them.

On the Monday morning the enemy could be seen very busy,
making intrenchments and throwing up field-works with great
skill, determined to dispute every inch of ground to the last.
The firing on both sides was continued very sharply all night.
They still kept throwing their balls into our camp. One of
them struck the ground close to my tent door, and drove the
earth over us inside and then bounded through the camp. We
could hear them coming several seconds before they reached us.
Being so far away they had to elevate the balls so high to throw
them into our camp, that we could hear them up in the air, as
if they were in the clouds. It was reported that they had but
one gun that would throw a ball into camp, and it was called
"long Tom." It was mounted upon the wall of the fort. Our
artillery played upon it to try to upset it.

A very remarkable thing happened on the morning of the
day here mentioned: twenty or thirty of our men were standing
together, talking, when a nine-pounder fell in the midst of
them, doing no harm to any one.

We were ordered to the front in the evening, to man the
intrenchments and occupy the advanced works; and as our
works were getting further advanced more troops were required
to occupy them, so the 52nd regiment of native infantry was
ordered to reinforce us. It was plain to be seen that if we
got on no faster than we did, we should be compelled to give up

through fatigue. In the first place, the party that had been relieved to get rest could not, through our camp being pitched so near, and the balls continually flying about us; and in the next place, we were not near strong enough, and the men were getting very impatient, and wanting to know why the general did not let them go into them, for the enemy grew very insolent. At twelve o'clock at night we got a dram of grog a man, and it was reported that the general intended to fight at day-break; and at three o'clock we were told that the report was true. We were to make an attack upon the two villages and their intrenchments, which we were to drive them from, and to occupy, that is, if wc were able. My comrade and I were talking it over, and thinking we should have as much as we could do, but he little knew his end was so near. It was what we might all expect, for it was certain some of us must fall. I felt very excited when I was thinking of my own fate. I thought I might not have many more hours to live.

CHAPTER VII.

AT half-past four o'clock on the morning of the 12th, the weather was very fine and clear, and by all appearance it was likely to be a very hot day. We were reinforced by a wing of the 10th regiment. At six o'clock, we had another dram of grog, and fresh reinforcements joined us from camp. Our cooks came with our breakfast, but we had not time to get any. Some of our men snatched a little as they went by, and ate it as they marched along. We formed up for the attack in close column, under shelter of a native temple. It was a large brick building, and surrounded by a large tope of trees. The balls came clashing through the trees, and cutting down the branches, which fell amongst us. The enemy appeared to be aware of our intention, for they kept up a galling fire; though they had done no hurt so far.

I had then some very curious feelings. I thought that I might be in eternity in a few minutes more, and how little I was prepared to meet my fate. I would have given the world, at that moment, to have been in England. I thought of the times I had been warned that death was sure, and now I felt that the time was come. All the wickedness I had done flashed across my mind in a moment, and I felt condemned to die. I tried to remember the prayers that my mother had taught me when a child; but we had no time for reflection, for we were not on the spot more than ten minutes before we were ordered to advance.

We were composed of about three thousand infantry, one troop of artillery, and one squadron of cavalry; the whole under the command of the colonel of my regiment, Colonel Potton, acting brigadier in place of brigadier Markham, who was wounded on the 10th. Out of this number of troops engaged, there were not more than one thousand Europeans, composed of one wing of my regiment, and one of the 10th regiment. The other half was in reserve, and guarding the camp. We were supported on the left by a portion of our allied troops, and our heavy artillery in battery kept up a constant fire, as long as they could, to keep the enemy in check, during the time we were forming up.

We advanced in close column of companies through the trees, and, as we got clear, we were exposed to the whole of the enemy's fire: but it was at a long distance for their musketry. We formed line to the left, which then brought us facing the villages. Our orders were to wait for the signal gun to fire. The enemy's fire was so dreadful that we were ordered to lie down, when the balls skimmed over us by thousands. The musket balls came shower after shower, cutting the grass off close to our heads, or burying themselves in the sand, close by; whilst the cannon shot was ploughing the earth up all round. I lay as close to the ground as I possibly could, expecting every moment that a ball would sink into my head. A thousand thoughts crossed my mind at this time, and it was so I saw with every other man. Our colonel had dismounted, and stood by his horse, talking and instructing his men, telling us to level low and keep together—to be cool and steady—and to act with judgment; but what surprised me most was, we could not see a man of the enemy. They had got behind their entrenchments, keeping up a most awful fire.

We had not lain more than five minutes, when my company was ordered to advance in extended order, to cover the line as it advanced, and engage the enemy's skirmishers. This was the light company. At this time we had not returned a shot, but kept it reserved, to make it tell when we did part

with it. As soon as the bugle sounded "the skirmish," we sprang
to our feet and extended. I felt the wind of several balls, and
quite expected one to go through me every moment. We took
cover behind some bushes and sand-hills, when the signal-gun
from the battery fired, and our bugles sounded "the advance" for
the whole line. Then every man sprang to his feet, and the
whole line advanced in good order.

We had not gone more than two hundred yards before we
came up to a nullah, or dry water-course. This was about five
yards across and twelve feet deep. It was so unlooked for that
it put the whole to a stand for a moment: but it was only for a
moment. British courage was not to be daunted at this; for
down it we went, my company leading the way, one pushing
another up the opposite side, while others were getting the
scaling ladders to cross with. One man was killed in crossing.
Now the poor infantry were left to themselves; for our cavalry
and artillery could not cross. As we rose on the bank, the
enemy's fire became dreadful, and several of our men began to
fall; but forward we rushed, and then the fight became general.
We scaled the walls of the village after some desperate fighting
in getting over. Several of our men were killed at the top.
Our colonel was among the foremost, cutting his way sword in
hand. My comrade was shot dead from beside me. He stood
on my right. The ball went through his breast. His name
was William Hanson; he came from a village against Bingham
in Nottinghamshire.

We soon made ourselves masters of the first village, but the
encounter was terrible, as the enemy were no cowards, nor
were they afraid of cold steel. Our dear old colonel was killed
here; but not till he had done good work. This village in our
possession, forward we rushed, driving the enemy before us to
the next, when we commenced a fierce attack. Our foes were
not idle, for they as fiercely returned it. This, like the other,
was walled all round, having a large temple in it, which was

well manned, and they did us some damage before we got possession. I was among the foremost at the door, and we had
something to do before we could force it open, which we did
with the butt ends of our muskets, whilst others scaled the
walls on the opposite side. They defended every inch of
ground most bravely; but we drove them from house to house,
leaving numbers of dead behind them. They fought most
desperately for the temple, for it was full of men. One of their
chief officers had taken up his quarters here. He and all the
men inside were killed; I believe not one escaped—they did
not ask for quarter and none was given.

The officer's name was Jhube Sing; he was kin to Moolraj,
and had charge of the advanced posts. Some papers of great
importance were found upon his body, which disclosed treachery
going on between Sheer Sing, our ally, and the enemy. This
was what was reported.

The fighting here was awful. What with the rolls of musketry, the clash of arms, and the shrieks, cries, and groans of
the wounded and dying, all was a dreadful scene of confusion.
In one place might be seen men in their last death-struggle,
grappling each other by the throat; while others were engaged
hand to hand with the deadly weapon, the bayonet, thrusting it
through each other's bodies, or blowing out each other's brains
—blood, brains, skin, skulls, and flesh, being all dashed in our
faces!

All fear had now left me. I never once thought of dying
myself, although numbers were falling all around. By ten
o'clock the village was fully in our possession, and we were
rushing forward after the flying enemy, up to their battery and
a long range of entrenchments they had thrown up, which was
well manned by resolute fellows. As soon as their own men
had got clear, they opened a galling fire from both batteries
and intrenchments upon us; and as we were in no kind of
order, we were compelled to throw ourselves down, to escape

such a destructive fire, and take shelter behind some sand-hills and trees. We were now in a very critical situation, not more than half of our men being here, part only having followed the enemy. The remainder were scattered in different parts of the village, and our ranks were broken. We were in no kind of order; and as for officers to give orders and restore order, I saw none. We were all ordering ourselves. We could see we were not able to go any further in this way. Where were our sepoys now it had come to the point? They never left the village; and we should have acted wisely if we had not; for several men's lives would have been saved, which were lost for no purpose. The truth of the matter was, our colonel was killed; and at this time very few knew to it,—so that the next officer in command dared not order us to retreat.

We had been in this situation for some time, when our bugles sounded—first the "assembly," next the "cease fire," then the "retreat;" so, what with one thing and what with another, we were almost bewildered. We therefore retreated, and took shelter in the village, where we found the remainder. During the time we were returning the enemy's fire, before we retreated, I saw several men fall. I had taken post behind a tree, which sheltered me from the balls of the enemy; but the tree had got it pretty well, for several had struck it. This tree had grown very well; it was forked about the height of my breast, so that I loaded and fired from it with good effect, for I sent my balls among them smartly. One of our 3rd company's sergeants came up to me, and said, "You have got a good place here—is there room for two?" As there was not, he knelt down at the back of a small sand-hill, which was close beside me, and commenced firing. He had not fired more than two rounds before a ball passed through his breast, and he fell back dead at my feet. His name was Douglas. One of my fellow corporals also fell, severely wounded; his name was Hitchcock. He belonged to my company; he came from Harby in Nottinghamshire.

.J

As soon as the enemy saw us withdraw into the village, they thought we were going to retreat altogether, so they let a yell out of them, and rushed boldly forward, flourishing their swords as they came near; but they met such a shower of our balls that it laid a number of them on their mother earth, and the remainder were glad to take shelter in their intrenchments. Again they made an attack, but were driven back. We were determined to hold the villages we had seized. During the time this was going on a detachment of our allied troops came rushing up on our left, following some of the enemy's stragglers, and as we did not know them from the enemy (being dressed so much alike) we fired into them in mistake, and several of the poor fellows were killed and wounded!

It was now generally known that our colonel was killed. Major Inglis therefore took command, and order was restored. The General came, and gave directions to us to keep possession of the ground and villages we had taken, and to level every hut and house with the ground, except one or two of the principal buildings, which we were to leave for shelter. Our sappers soon set to work, and some they blew up, and some were burnt. Large quantities of ammunition were also found, which we destroyed.

We collected our dead and buried them, whilst those of the enemy we set fire to in heaps, as they lay, the roads being fairly choked up with the bodies. It was a shocking sight to see the flesh burning and all in flames, whilst the blood and other matter was running along the ground; but cruel as this may appear, it is nothing more than the custom of the country calls for. They were most of them of the Hindoo caste, and they always burn their dead; but the stench was unbearable.

I saw our Colonel's body; it lay under, or rather among about a dozen of the enemy, in a small square yard, in front of some half-dozen huts. It was maimed in several places; his wrist was cut nearly off, and on one side of his head was a deep cut. A musket ball had passed through his body. He looked noble even in death. The whole regiment lamented his loss. I also saw the body of our quarter-master. A musket ball had passed through his body; he was in great agony before he died, for about half an hour; he bit the ground, and tore up the sand with his hands. He had been married but about four months, to a very excellent young lady. His last words were "Oh, my dear wife, tell her all I have is hers; tell her my last words were for her."

This action was now ended; but still we kept up a constant fire at each other at long distances. It was about eleven o'clock, so we had had five hours downright hard work. The field all round presented a most awful sight of the wreck of the action. Broken arms of all description lay strewed all round, with dead men and horses. The village was but a heap of ruins.

The enemy appeared to be getting round to our right at about 12 o'clock. My company (the grenadiers) and No. 3 company were ordered to take possession of a group of huts standing among a few trees, which the enemy had abandoned, and was now trying to recover. They stood about 600 yards to our right and front. To get possession of the huts, we must needs be exposed to the whole range of the enemy's fire; for we must cross a piece of ground entirely open to them. Our only plan, therefore, was to form in sections, and double across as fast as possible, which we did. No sooner did the enemy see us, than they opened a furious fire upon us from their batteries and intrenchments. I saw one cannon shot go through one man's body, carry away another's leg, and severely wound a third. The balls came faster than ever I witnessed them before; but they appeared to fire very high, most of them going over our heads. However, we got possession.

A very remarkable thing happened to one of my company, named Mitchell. Having a watch in his pocket, a ball struck it, and broke it, but saved his life. A ball passed through another man's cap. They directed their fire upon these huts all the remaining part of the day; still, they could not succeed in dislodging us.

At one o'clock we got some food and grog. I felt very ill all day, being feverish, and my head aching from excitement.

I do not know the whole loss on our side, but as near as I can say it was 50 killed, and 100 wounded, making a total of about 150, or upwards. The loss of my regiment was as follows;—two officers killed, nine men killed, four officers wounded, thirty-two men wounded. Total, killed and wounded, forty-seven.

The names of our officers, killed and wounded :—Lieutenant Colonel Potton (killed), Quarter-master Taylor (killed), Captain Balfour (severely wounded, dying afterwards), Captain King (wounded), Lieutenant Birdwhistle (wounded), Ensign Swinburn (wounded). Major Mondesember of the tenth regiment was killed at the same place as our colonel; he was a fine, tall-looking man, well respected by his regiment. He was buried with our colonel and quarter-master.

CHAPTER VIII.

THE RETREAT.

TOWARDS evening we commenced to extend our intrenchments up to the villages, and to throw up a battery to play upon the enemy's, and their field works. They kept up a sharp fire all the day.

At dark we got more guns into play. I saw one of our shots strike one of the enemy's guns, and, completely dismounting it, send one of the men that was working it flying into the air. This was hailed with a cheer from the British army. My company and the other three which had been engaged, were ordered to the rear, as a reserve for the night. We took up a position behind a sand-hill, for cover, and out of musket-shot. However, we were not out of cannon-shot, for the enemy had got our range, and continued pitching shot amongst us all night, at intervals, but the sand-hill stood our friend pretty well, as the balls struck the top and did no more harm than cover us over with sand. We stood to our arms several times during the night, the enemy making various feigned attacks, but being met by such a steady fire that they deemed it prudent to retire to a respectful distance.

As we lay here I could not but admire our shells, as they took their flight into the air from our batteries, the fusee attached to them showing the direction they were taking, as they went whirling over and over. They then fell down with force into the city, and dreadful would be the effects of the explosion to those persons who were near the spot.

On Wednesday, the 13th, at daylight, we were ordered to camp, to get a little rest and food; but of the former we had little, and of food we got some, such as it was.

At dusk we were ordered to the advance posts again, where we remained all night, extending our works, the firing on both sides being kept up very sharply, and the enemy being very daring. We had three killed and four wounded. Our shells blew up two or three of the enemy's ammunition waggons, and I think we did pretty good execution, as they became venture-some.

On the next day we were relieved in the morning at day-break. Several more men were killed and wounded. The enemy was gaining courage, and something very strange was going on; but our General kept everything very secret. Still, he could not help seeing that his handful of men was worn out with fatigue and hardship, and the siege not yet com-menced.

Our work, too, was not as it was when we began. Our intrenchments and outposts, being further advanced, took all our force to occupy them; so that we were obliged to leave a very weak guard in camp, which was very dangerous, for if the enemy had but known it, they could have attacked our camp and blown up our magazines. Then we should have been at their mercy, whilst we well knew they would in such a case kill every man of us.

About nine o'clock in the evening we were doomed to hear bad news, which, alas! was too true: Sheer Sing, with 7000 men, and from six to nine guns, deserted us and joined the enemy. This man was a native prince, and was sent in command of those troops (our allies) by the Lahore Govern-ment. He had been suspected to be dealing treacherously for some days before. He intended to fall upon our camp in the rear, whilst it was so weakly guarded; but he was repulsed in this treacherous scheme. This news spread like wild-fire through the camp, although our General tried to keep it as secret as possible, for fear it should dishearten his men; but it was impossible for him to deceive us. We were worn

out with fatigue, faint, hungry, and discouraged. We had
had no rest since the 7th—the day the siege was raised; and
now we were deserted, and were but a handful of men, to
contend with a host of savage enemies. So we could but
fight and die; for we had no reinforcements at hand.

Our officers looked dark and melancholy, and things appeared to be at a stand-still. I received two letters from
England in the evening; one recording the death of my
youngest sister. Troubles were all coming at once; but I
never make troubles of what cannot be helped.

I mounted the artillery park guard in the evening, and
was sitting upon the trail of one of the guns, reading the
contents of my letters, just as it was getting dark, when our
colonel (Brooks) came at full speed along the camp, crying,
"The enemy is coming on the right." All in a moment what
a change of scene! Bugles sounding; the alarm drums
beating to arms; men and officers running;—all was confusion
and hurry. The artillerymen were loading and running the
guns up to the front; the cavalry mounting, and men falling
into their ranks. It would be impossible to describe the scene
for the moment; though it was only for a moment. All were
soon ready and under arms, waiting for further orders. A
British army is always ready, and is very seldom taken by
surprise. The officer of my guard sent me out to reinforce
my sentinels, and to form the remainder of the guard up to
support the guns (or, I might as well state the truth, which
I am almost ashamed to do—it was the sergeant and I who
did this, for the officer was drunk, and did not know what he was
doing). This officer was sometime after tried by a court-
martial, and whilst awaiting the sentence of the court, he died
frenzied with liquor.

This alarm happily turned out to be false, for in a few
inutes after another officer came, an aide-de-camp, with an
order for "turn in." It appeared that our cavalry picquet

and a cavalry patrol of the enemy had come in contact with each other, when our men charged the enemy, causing a jingling of accoutrements, and clatter of horses' hoofs, which led the inlying picquet to believe that the enemy was advancing in force to the attack, and they gave the alarm; it being then so dark that they could not see.

Continual alarms occurred all night, and sharp firing of musketry from our advanced posts. We withdrew our guns from battery, and most of our siege equipage, before daylight. The enemy grew more daring; they appeared at a loss to know what we were at, and were continually patrolling close up to us, which led to a deal of useless firing.

On Friday, the 15th, we remained quiet all day, doing nothing except keeping our ground. Reports got about that we were to retire, and it was quite clear that we should be compelled to do so before long.

Our General gave orders that evening that no fires were to be lighted during the night, and as little noise made as possible; and that as soon as it was completely dark, we were to strike our camp, and pack up our baggage quietly, and to be ready to march at any moment, but where we did not know.

A strong guard was sent to the front, to occupy the outposts during the night, with orders to deceive the enemy as much as possible, and to keep them in check, by continuing a brisk fire wherever they shewed themselves. They watched every movement very closely, and appeared very suspicious, and examined every inch of ground very closely. They guessed we had abandoned our intrenchments, and laid mines to blow them up. If they had only known our situation, they would have had no need to be so very cautious, for they might have cut us all up.

I must now describe the state and feelings of our little band. All hands now knew the condition we were left in,—deserted, weary, and worn out with fatigue. We had never had a good

meal of food. We were faint, and looked more like moving
skeletons than men; and after our long toil, and the sacrifice of
a number of valuable lives, some of our bravest men had here
fallen uselessly. All this produced a great impression upon
the men's minds. We were obliged to leave everything to the
enemy. All seemed lost: even our chief officers looked downcast. All felt as though we had but one thing to do, and that
was to fight and die. The feeling among the men was, rather
to die than leave a single gun in the hands of the enemy. I
believe it was as brave a little army as ever took the field.

Several alarms were given during the night, and one young
soldier left the outpost, and came into camp, abandoning his
company. He was very near being tried for cowardice, but he
got off with being tried for quitting the field without leave.

On Saturday, the 16th, at four o'clock, a.m., everything was
ready to move off. All the men were ordered to leave the
outposts as still as possible, and to join us when all was
reported ready. We commenced our retreat, not knowing
where we were going to, leaving a number of shell behind, as
some of our camels had died, and some had been captured by
the enemy. We were therefore compelled to leave them, they
being of no use to the enemy.

It was still dark, and about four o'clock a.m., or as near that
as we could judge. The morning was fine, and the stars
twinkled brightly as they studded the clear sky. All was as
still as death, as we were waiting for the words " quick march"
to be given. Something like a deathlike silence pervaded us—
not the sound of a shot was to be heard, nor the loud booming
of cannon. It was an awful moment of time! God knows
what each mind was thinking of!—for the very word "retreat,"
to a British army is like poison: it is hurtful to the soldier's
mind. *Retreat!* We think of it with disdain. The people of
England would read in the papers that the army at Mooltan
were compelled to give up the siege and retreat. I believe

K

there was not a man there, but would not have returned and died fighting, rather than leave with the word *retreat!* But we must obey the command of our General, and we had not the least doubt that he was doing all for the best, to save his little band from complete destruction.

In a few minutes the words, " quick march " were given, and the whole moved off. My company was ordered out in extended order, to cover the right flank, and engage the enemy's skirmishers, should they follow; but not to fire, except we were hard pressed. We wound our way through the bush, meeting with no resistance, and saw no enemy following. We were flattering ourselves that we were getting away unperceived; but as daylight began to break in a very short time, we heard the sound of shots in our rear, which gradually increased. The enemy had got our scent, and were after us. The firing took place with the rear guard of cavalry, though the enemy did not press us very hard: for as daylight dawned we could see nothing but a few cavalry following, to the number of a few hundreds, and they kept at a respectful distance. After following three or four miles, our cavalry showed them a front, which they did not think well to face, and they left us to ourselves. We proceeded very slowly, having to cut our way through some of the sand-hills and bush, to draw our heavy guns through. We passed through our allied camp, under the command of Lieut. Edwardes. They were in a good position, with a large intrenchment all round, and good batteries. It would take the enemy sometime to dislodge them. We halted at ten o'clock, and pitched our camp at night. We were not far from the city. We took our route a long way round to reach the south side. I should think we were not more than four or five miles from Mooltan. We could see the tops of the temples very plainly.

We were now on the left of our allied troops. What the General could see in taking up ground here was a mystery to

me and a many more. The nature of the ground was not calculated for an army on the defensive by a great deal. There
was no natural defence, no shelter nor protection. Far different;
all round was a complete thick jungle, which we were not at all
acquainted with; and we had pitched our camp in the centre.

The day had been very hot, and we had been engaged till
dark, cutting and clearing a place to pitch our camps upon, so
it was late before we had any refreshment. The water was so
bad that we were obliged to stop our breath whilst we drank
it; no other could be got, so that we were obliged to use it.

CHAPTER IX.

THE RETREAT AND THE BATTLE.

ON Sunday, September the 17th, we were employed in cutting the jungle and clearing the ground for our camp. It was dreadfully hot, as no wind could get to us. There was not a breath of air stirring; and the snakes and scorpions were numberless. We were always in danger. Troops of jackalls were also howling about the camp all night, and ready to devour us before our time.

From the 17th up to the 21st, each day was spent alike, the enemy hovering about our front, and exchanging a few shots with our picquet. On the last-named day, the enemy were diverting themselves in front of our camp, but at a great distance; they did not come within shot. On the two following days we perceived something in the sun like a round, dark, substance, about the size of a six-pound shot.

The enemy made their appearance, on the 24th, in full force, with cavalry, infantry, and artillery, in front of us. We expected they were coming to the attack. Our camp was in an alarm. One division was ordered out, whilst the remainder were ordered to stand to arms in the centre of the camp. As soon as they saw us advancing to meet them, the cowardly rascals showed us their backs; but they came back after we had turned in, and were patrolling along the front of our position. Our mounted videttes exchanged a few shots with them, but towards five o'clock in the evening they brought some guns to bear upon our camp. One man of the 51st regiment was killed, and one wounded, in their tents. The ball passed through the camp. Most of their balls fell short, and did not reach us. We turned out to face them, but, as before, they turned and showed us their backs. Our cavalry charged, though, on account of the irregular nature of the ground, and a number of dry water-courses, they could do no good, and so came back. It made the enemy quiet all night. We stood to arms all night, for we expected an attack from them. A party composed of cavalry, artillery, and infantry, was ordered out to the front, to meet them, and give them a warm reception; but no enemy made their appearance.

On the 25th, they were patrolling along the front, as if they wanted to take some advantage of us. If they had any shame, they ought to have been ashamed; for they were a cowardly set. If we could but have made one good charge at them, we should have made some of them rue, as our men were mad to get at them. Our General, too, found that he had taken up bad ground; he therefore ordered a retreat.

We struck camp on the following day, at four o'clock, a.m., and marched at five. We were followed by the enemy very closely. Our cavalry charged them and drove them back with loss; so that they kept at a more respectful distance. We did not go far (about two miles) before we took up a strong position, good by nature. A range of sand-hills ran along our front, which we occupied as our advance posts. We had several batteries of heavy guns mounted upon them, having good command along the front, which was a very thick jungle; but on the left it was more open, with several topes of palm trees, and the ruins of several small mud villages; and about four or five miles further away, the river Ravee ran, joining the Sutlej a few miles further down. On the right we communicated with the allied troops, and the rear of our camp was more open than the front; though there were large patches of jungle. We had a battery of field artillery. The road from Baalpoor to Mookan also came by our rear, which was our only road of retreat, if compelled; and the only communication we had.

The rajah ol Baalpoor was allied to the British, and assisted in our operations with what he had, such as escorting our convoys and supplies with his troops; and he sent some to join the allied camp; but they were of little use—they knew no discipline, and were very badly equipped, so that they only served to make up a number. If he had turned traitor, our communication would have been cut off completely, and our doom would have been utter ruin.

We were very badly off for water, and the ground our camp was pitched upon was very uneven, being full of large bushes.

Between the 27th and October the 3rd, we were harassed by the enemy (who captured our post, with letters and despatches from England); and we became short of water. Our rations also became short and bad.

Several prisoners were brought into camp on the latter day, having been captured by our cavalry. We found a job for all; for they were sent out to the front, under a guard of sepoys, to set fire to the jungle, to burn and clear the front of our camp, so that we might have a clear view.

On the morning of the 9th, Sheer Sing left Mooltan with all his troops; he struck his camp at an early hour, and was marching up the right bank of the river Ravee. All our cavalry and artillery were ordered out to pursue, but he had got too far before our spy could get away without being perceived, to let us know, so that the troops were ordered back to camp. As he had got so far, it was thought dangerous to follow him, but had we known at the time he left, we could have given him a dressing.

Let it be remembered that this man deserted us the preceding month, with all the men under his command. Upwards of 300 of his men surrendered themselves on the 9th, to Lieut. Edwardes, in command of the allied troops. They all laid down their arms and gave up. They were all Mussulmen. They were sworn to be faithful to the British cause, but we could not place any confidence in them. We made out the cause of Sheer Sing's parting from the Dewan Moolraj, by the craft of Lieut. Edwardes and the General. Lieut. Edwardes wrote a letter in the native language, and bribed a man to take it to Moolraj. It was written and directed to Sheer Sing, in friendly terms, telling him to get into the city, and then fall upon the Dewan, and we were to be ready to take the advantage and storm the place. Moolraj got the letter (which it was intended he should) and read it. Believing it to be true, it caused him to be jealous of Sheer Sing, and he accused him of treachery. This made them part. It was just what we wanted; but the intention of the General was, to destroy his army when he parted, and it was very badly arranged that we did not, as he afterwards proved the greatest enemy we had. He collected a very large army as he marched up the country, inducing whole regiments to join him, at one time, from the Lahore Government, of cavalry, artillery, and infantry.

I saw a man's leg cut off on the 12th, the first I had seen under the operation of chloroform. He never stirred the least under the operation, and knew nothing of what was going on. He said, after he came to himself again, that he felt nothing, nor did he know it was off until he looked. He was wounded on the 12th of September, by a ball through the knee. Our officers were very kind to the wounded; they did all in their power for them, and gave them anything they had.

The General reviewed the whole of the troops under his command on the morning of the 13th, and gave the whole great credit for general good and orderly conduct, in camp and in the field.

Our men looked very bad for want of proper food. Our living was dreadful. The hospital was getting full, and men were dying every day, from nothing but want; our living consisting of very bad mutton and boiled rice. The sheep at the best of times are bad, and what could they be then, when it took six of them to weigh ninety lbs. They were nothing but skin and bone.

Our men said that we often ate dead dogs for sheep, which I was inclined to believe; for they were about our camp by hundreds. They were the native dogs, most of them of a brown or dark brown colour. We got a little flour sometimes, though of the coarsest kind—so coarse, that we could not stick it together, to make a cake. Hunger is a sharp thorn, and pricked so deep then, that it made me think—

> Loved land! though I roam on a far distant shore,
>   My thoughts and my heart are in thee;
> I live in the hope of returning once more
>   To the land of the brave and the free!
> My knapsack shall grace my parents' blest cot,
>   And my story shall cause a glad tear;
> Nor shall British India e'er be forgot,
>   Or Old England—the land I love dear!

On the 14th of October, the half of each regiment, with the whole of the cavalry and horse artillery, were ordered out very early, as a reconnoitring party, to reconnoitre the enemy's position, and see if they had thrown up any fresh works.

We proceeded to the north-west side of the city and fort, meeting no opposition; for it was as yet dark. We were close under the fort walls, when daylight broke; and as we had marched with as little noise as possible, they did not hear us. We (or at least our advanced guard) were not more than 500 yards from the fort walls when the enemy perceived us. No sooner were we seen than a signal gun was fired to alarm the garrison, and a number of cannon shots came whizzing amongst us, but did us no damage, and we soon got out of reach. Their cavalry came pouring out, and attempted to get in our rear, but were repulsed in the attempt, by our cavalry and horse artillery dashing to the rear and charging. Unluckily, however, when they got within about 100 yards of the enemy they came up to a nullah, which they could not pass, and so were obliged to content themselves with exchanging a few random shots. They made several attempts to cut off our retreat as we were coming back. We arrived at camp at eleven o'clock.

The country all round this part of the town was beautiful. There were a number of splendid gardens, full of all kinds of fruit trees and native noblemen's mansions, and very fine temples ; and all round was scattered with hundreds of date-trees, presenting a grand and truly Indian picture.

We captured two convoys of salt, going to the city. It is famous for its commerce in this article, and derives therefrom its chief revenue.

About fifty of my regiment, and the same number of the 10th regiment, now commenced the gun drill. This was done because we had not artillerymen sufficient, so that they should be ready, if required for that purpose.

Moolraj was very kind : he set one of the 72nd regiment native infantry at liberty. He was taken on the night of Sept. 9th, when colonel Pottoun made the attack upon the villages. He stated that the Dewan was very kind, and would have set the other men at liberty; but they could not walk, as their wounds were not well, and one of them died. He said that they had everything they liked, such as there was in the fort. (This was a bit of policy of the Dewan, because he knew that we were waiting for reinforcements.)

He said that they were making more intrenchments, and throwing up fresh redoubts, and cutting down the trees, and levelling the large sand-hill on which he had a battery that pitched the shot into our camp. He was aware, if we got it into our possession, we could take shelter from their shot behind it, and also plant our batteries upon it, as it had a command over the town.

Some stores arrived on the 22nd, including bedding, which we stood in great need of, for we very nearly lay upon the bare sand, and the nights became very cold. They brought a few

L

pairs of trousers, but not sufficient to supply the whole, for half
the men had to patch theirs with leather, or any coloured cloth.
Money was also brought up to pay the men with. Our colonel
had sent for some bottles of ale and porter for the regiment,
which also arrived. This was such a thing as was never heard
of in this part of the country before : it all came up from Calcutta, upwards of 2000 miles away. We gave at the rate of
10d. per bottle, and the officers paid the remainder of the expense, which was very kind of them. The whole came from
Ferozepoor, escorted by a detachment of troops, composed of
upwards of a thousand men, of the different regiments lying in
camp, who were left behind, sick and weakly, at the time we
took the field. Having now got better they were ordered up to
join their regiments. About thirty came for my regiment.

More stores arrived on the morning of the 23rd. They said
they saw nothing of the enemy up the way. Some native
merchants came with them, with flour, and tobacco, and many
other things for sale.

English pipes cost four-pence each. All their eatables were
soon devoured, dear as they sold them. Next day our cooks
ran away, so we were in a worse mess than ever; and what was
worse than all, they took the coppers with them, and left us
nothing to cook with. I expected they would have gone before,
as they were as badly off as we for food. I did not blame them,
for they were under no compulsion to stop.

We could see some mountains to the left and front of our
camp on the morning of the 27th. They were a range running
from the Affghanistan mountains down into the Scinde country.
The weather was getting very cool, and the air in this country
is always the clearest at this time of the year. Our men were
dying very fast, from want of proper food. The hospital was
full; it was an awful sight to see the poor fellows lying upon
the brink of eternity.

My constitution is like a horse's; for no matter whatever it was, be it ever so rough, I could eat it. The flour that I bought to make a cake of, had in it straw an inch long, and was full of chaff and dirt of every description. We soon made a graveyard. At the back of our camp might be seen numbers of fresh heaps of earth, beneath which were as many or more human bodies. I wished an end was put to the war either by a battle or a retreat.

On the 28th, the enemy's cavalry were hovering about our front, and became so daring that our cavalry were ordered out; but the cowardly dogs retreated as soon as they saw the latter advance towards them.

Our engineers tried their rockets, but they proved to be damaged, and were quite useless. The enemy were to be seen patrolling the front on the 29th; and two of our officers were very near being captured by some of their patrol. They were riding in the front of the camp, when the enemy dropped upon them unperceived, and they only made their escape by the swiftness of their horses. The enemy still showed themselves in large numbers on the day following. They appeared to want to be at some mischief, and keep the camp in a continual alarm. Our cavalry made several attempts to bring them to receive a charge, but in vain. Our cavalry and the enemy's had a skirmish on the 31st. The enemy got rather too bold, and came too near, when our cavalry made a dashing charge, and overtook the hindermost, making them pay for their trouble.

CHAPTER X.

ACTIVE WARFARE.

WITH the commencement of a new month (November), our enemy commenced a fresh plan of operations, on a more determined scale.

The enemy's cavalry came in large bodies on the morning of the 1st, very early, and became bolder and more determined than ever. Still, they acted with great caution. Something was going on more than we were aware of. At ten o'clock they formed a large body of cavalry, immediately up in our front, as if about to make a charge into our camp. The whole of our cavalry were ordered to mount; one battery of field artillery, and one squadron of cavalry, advanced to the attack, but the enemy steadily withdrew, as if to draw ours on. The infantry were only lookers-on. At eleven o'clock the enemy opened a heavy fire of artillery from the extreme right, which did not surprise us much, as we judged that they were at some secret movement. They sent the balls thick about our camp; but our artillery had orders to open fire from the heavy battery with shell, which had a good effect, destroying a number of our enemy, and compelling them to retire. They had not calculated that our heavy shell could reach them, but it was far superior to theirs. They took up a fresh position behind a dry watercourse or river, more to the right, nearer to Lieutenant Edwardes' camp, and out of reach of our guns. It was worse for our allies, for our foes could pitch their shot into their camp, and killed a number of them. They had their guns planted behind the embankment, so that our allies could not do any good, their shot not reaching the enemy.

About twelve o'clock, the day being fine, and the sun shining beautifully, the hand of death began to be busy, and ready to carry off its prey, by means of the different instruments which were glaring in the rays of the sunshine.

While this was going on upon the right, the enemy's cavalry was mustering in full force upon our left, and advancing fearlessly. Our cavalry were ordered out, with two troops of horse artillery, the whole of the infantry to stand to arms. Our cavalry advanced to the charge, but the enemy retired. They came again and again the same way, and each time retired, never receiving a charge, which was very aggravating.

At one o'clock, the enemy's cavalry were seen in large numbers, turning our left flank. Our cavalry were ordered to remount. At this time I stood upon a sand-hill, and could see all that was going on. Our cavalry divided into two wings, the right and left; the left were ordered to keep retiring, and drawing the enemy on, while the right had orders to take a circuitous route to gain the enemy's rear, which they obeyed to the letter, and formed up, concealed by some brushwood. The left wing had played their part well; they diverted the enemy's attention, and drew them well round the flank. Now came "threes about," and "charge"; and charge they did in good style! As soon as the enemy saw them coming, they retreated at full speed; and our left wing after them, at full gallop, when a regular chase took place. The game had been well played on our part.

It was a scene worth describing, to see the right wing, which had been concealed, come dashing out, and fully meet the enemy in their speedy retreat. They were now obliged to stand, for they could not get away; and regular cutting and slashing took place for a few minutes. The enemy got away as soon as they could; but not until a number were killed and wounded. Such a charge I never before nor since have witnessed. I saw their swords flash in the sunlight as they cut at each other, and both man and horse were hurled to the

ground with the greatest fury. I saw two of our men (natives),
who had had their horses killed under them, come running into
camp.   They were in good spirits; and when I asked them how
things were going on, they replied in their language, "we have
killed plenty."   The enemy made their escape as fast as they
could, our men following them at full speed, cutting them
down wherever they came up to them.   How many men the
enemy lost is not known, but a great many were killed,
wounded, and taken prisoners.   Our men brought two of the
enemy's officers' heads in with them, as trophies.

The loss on our side was only trifling, being seven men
wounded (one mortally), and two horses killed, and a number
wounded.   The enemy got such a dressing on the left, that
they never again shewed themselves in that quarter.   This was
not the case, however, on the right; for the enemy were giving
it our allied troops very severely.   They kept up a very heavy
fire of cannon, and killed a number of them in their camp;
while the shot from the guns of the allies could not do the
enemy any harm.   The enemy's shot could not reach our part
of the camp, although they tried all in their power to do so.
Things now appeared to be turning altogether; for, instead of
our being the besieging army, we had become the besieged.
Very dark looks were to be seen among our head men, and
they were often heard to express a wish that the Bombay
army would join us.

At five o'clock in the evening, part of my brigade, and the
sappers and engineers, were ordered to the front as a working
party, to throw up intrenchments, and a battery of our heavy
guns; so, taking cover of the bushwood, and favoured by the
darkness, we proceeded on our work, with pickaxes and shovels
upon our shoulders, and muskets in our hands, until we got
close up to the enemy.   They heard us, and fired several shots
in the direction where we were; but as they could not tell what
we were at, they acted with great caution.   At one time they

tried all they could to draw out our fire, so as to see whereabouts we were, but without success. They once came within
a very few yards of our covering party. We could hear them
talking very plainly, and we could hear their relief, going to relieve their sentinels. We had one man killed and several
wounded. By daylight we had a good battery of guns ready,
and an intrenchment thrown up; and as soon as daylight broke,
our battery opened fire, which no little surprized the enemy.
A good fire of muskets was also kept upon the enemy wherever
they showed themselves; but through working so hard during
the night, and being so weak, we were completely worn out.

On the 4th, my company turned out for the intrenchments.
We worked by night, and occupied them by day. I was ordered to remain in camp, being orderly corporal, to get the men's
rations cooked, and take their breakfast (such as it was, for I believe a dog in England would not have touched it). In the morning I prepared as good a breakfast as I could to take to my company, composed of bread and rice, boiled, and some pieces of mutton (or I might say, skin and bone), and boiled coffee, which I put
into a large earthen vessel, and pressed three of our camp-followers to carry it upon their heads. They were unwilling to
go, but I took my musket in my hand, and fixed my bayonet;
and I compelled them to go, telling them, at the same time, that
our cooks had gone away, and that they must do it, for it was
war time, and there was no law if I shot them. When we had got
near to our outpost, the balls began to fly very fast, and whizzed
by very thickly; when at last the followers dropped down behind
a bank, and said they dared not go any further, adding that if a
ball struck one, and he was killed, our men would say, "never
mind, it's only a black man." I got them a little further, and
as the balls came so thickly, and they begged so hard, I left
them squatted behind a bank, while I went forward and brought
two of my company with me for the breakfast. One of the
sergeants of my company had just been slightly wounded the

ball went through his trowsers, and cut a bit of flesh off across his body. Our men were ready to worry their breakfasts, and as they sat in the intrenchments eating it, the balls came whizzing off the embankment, serving for music at meals.

I here make a remark concerning a native soldier belonging to the rifle company of the 72nd regiment of native infantry. He got over the embankment, and stood behind a bush, concealed as much as possible, and had killed at least five of the enemy; for every shot he fired a man fell. Some of my company told him he had better come into the intrenchment, or the enemy would pick him off; but encouraged by his good luck, he stuck to his post, and said it was "very good." He had scarcely said the words, before a ball sank into his head, and he fell back a corpse. He had well revenged his death.

The firing on both sides was kept up all day on the 5th, fiercer than ever. We were getting the worst of it now. Our allies, too, were becoming dissatisfied; for we learned that 150 of them had deserted during the night and joined the enemy; and no wonder, as the enemy's balls killed numbers in their camp. They could pitch them where they liked, killing the men in their tents; and our men were as much dissatisfied, from want of rest and food. The general feeling among the men was to fight: they might as well die fighting as be picked off by odd ones, as they were, and getting no forwarder. There was a general murmur through the whole camp. For want of sleep we were so overpowered sometimes, that we dropped off as we manned the intrenchments, when salvo after salvo from our batteries roused us up again.

At dusk in the evening we were ordered out as a working party for the night. We marched cautiously along until we arrived at our post, for another night of toil, with our accoutrements upon us. The murmur had become louder than ever amongst our men. We relieved a party of the 10th, who had one man wounded by a cannon shot, and the enemy (as the

moon shone dimly and our front was thickly dotted over with
bushes) approached close up to us; and every shovelful of earth
we threw up they could see, and a number of balls would come
whizzing at it. We cast a number of shovels-full up together
sometimes on purpose to make them fire; whilst others would
hold their caps upon their shovels, and there were sure to
be five or six balls come whizzing at them.

We had not as yet returned a bullet; but our battery kept in
full play all night, which was as readily returned by the enemy.
Our shot might as well have been saved, for the position the
enemy had taken was so well sheltered by the canal bank, that
our shot did them no harm. Our shell had been better, two of
the enemy's ammunition waggons having been blown up, and a
number of men killed besides.

They got so daring towards morning that we were obliged to
return them a few shots, by way of warning them to keep at a
respectful distance; and we were ordered to stand to our arms
twice. Their batteries became more galling than ever. The
balls came and struck the top of our works, covering us over
with earth, or burying themselves in the embankment, or ploughing up the earth where they fell over us.

I had a very narrow escape on one occasion, as I was throwing some earth up over the bank of the intrenchment. Ball after
ball came whizzing at me, and I could tell that the man who
fired must be close to me; so I determined on exchanging a
shot with him. I therefore mounted the bank, and took a cautious view all around, but could see no one. I had only just
taken my head away when a ball struck the very place where it
had been, and cut a hole through the sand, filling my eyes and
mouth, and covering my cap. "Eh!" said one of my compan
ions, "that's a good miss; you will never be killed after that;"
and I thought I was lucky too.

On Monday the 6th, we left a guard of five companies to man
the intrenchments, composed of two companies of my regiment,

M

and three companies of the 72nd regiment of native infantry, with
a portion of European and native artillery at the guns, the whole
not numbering 500 men—a small portion to keep a whole army
in check.

By the time we arrived at our camp we heard the firing at
the intrenchments increase, but at first we took no notice. As,
however, it continued to increase until it became a regular roll
of musketry—roll after roll, and salvo after salvo from the batteries—plainly telling us that the enemy had made an attack,
our bugle sounded " the alarm," and we were all under arms in
less than five minutes, and poured up in quarter distance column,
ready and willing to go forward. We had received no order to
do so, but the men became so impatient, that we were almost
come to the determination to go to the assistance of our comrades. There we stood, and only one or two officers joined us ;
when, at length, our gallant major, Inglish, came and told us
it was more than he dared do to tell us to go forward, being
obliged to wait until he received orders from the General. Our
colonel (Brooks) then came up and said, he thought it was nothing more than a little increase of firing ; but the men spoke
out plainly, and the cry was, " Let us go forward, for the outposts are attacked "; and the whole of the men became so furious
that the officers were obliged to beg them to remain, urging that
if it was anything serious we should soon be sent for. However, we had not stood here long before the truth was soon told,
as we saw some wounded men brought in ; and the first that
came was a much-respected officer, a captain of the 72nd regiment
of native infantry, severely wounded in the groin. He afterwards
died. A great number more came in one after another ; and
the firing began to slacken. A man then came running into
camp, out of breath, with an order for a fresh supply of ammunition to be sent off immediately. He also stated that the enemy had been beaten back, but that our men had fired all their
ammunition away, and that a reinforcement of the 10th regiment

had arrived to their assistance. We were sent to our tents again, to remain with our accoutrements upon us, ready to turn out at a moment's notice.

The attack was as follows, as correctly as I can give it from one of my companions. As soon as daylight came, the enemy made an attack upon our position, charging the intrenchments and batteries with great fury. Our men were rather taken by surprise. They saw a European at the head of a number of native troops, and supposing them to be a portion of our allies, under Edwardes, allowed them to approach quite close before they found out their mistake. Our men said he had white trousers, 'and a red jacket, and uniform cap on; but he was a Frenchman, and had played his part well. Though some one discovered the party to be the enemy and opened fire, even our officers ordered the men to cease fire, telling them they were our allies; but the latter began to open a heavy fire on our men, which soon convinced our officers they were enemies. They charged up to the very verge of our works, when our men rushed out and met them, and drove them back. Our men in their turn were driven back into the intrenchments again, and again did this handful of brave men repeat the charge, pushing the enemy back, and even entering their battery. They were so overpowered by numbers, however, that they were repulsed with loss. Two poor fellows were left, and cut up before their eyes. The enemy filled their mouths and ears full of powder, and then blew open their heads, and afterwards cut them limb from limb. One of these men was a fine young fellow, about nineteen years of age. His name was Jacob Daws: he came from the Meadow Platts, Nottingham. He was severely wounded, and two men had got him between them, bringing him with them; but as the enemy pressed them so hard, he begged them to leave him and save themselves, which they were obliged to do.

The enemy now, in larger numbers than ever, drove our men

into the intrenchments, and even some of them got into our battery, when the artillerymen drew their swords, and defended their guns. Notwithstanding their overwhelming force, our little band determined, rather than give up their post, to die upon the spot; and again drove the enemy back into their own works, yet not without some desperate fighting. Indeed, had the enemy repeated the charge, and the re-inforcements been a little longer before they arrived, all our men must have been killed; for they had not a single shot left to fire. The enemy appeared to have had enough, and ought to be ashamed; since they must have had at least 7000 men in the field against 500. They left their dead scattered all over the field. Their loss was great. Our men said that the three companies of native troops belonging to the 72nd regiment fought as well as any British. Our loss was, of my regiment, 10 killed and 20 wounded; 72nd regiment of native infantry 9 killed and 18 wounded; total 57. A number of these died of their wounds afterwards. This was all done in a very short time—not more than half an hour. It shows the struggle was desperate. The General went to see what had been done, when to his great astonishment, he saw ten dead men lying upon the bank of the trench.

The firing was continued all day on both sides, as usual. The sight of our killed and wounded so enraged the men, that our spirits fairly boiled for revenge. Things had now come to their worst pitch. Despair was in every countenance. We were worn out with fatigue and clammed; and with thin faces we looked more fit for the grave than the battle. I expected that the men would turn up and mutiny; they were only appeased by the colonel telling them that the General would be sure to let them fight on the morrow.

At 5 o'clock in the afternoon a council of war was summoned, composed of field-officers, to meet at the General's tent at seven, to come to a determination what measures were to be taken

to drive the enemy from their position. They came to a con-
clusion that we were to fight next morning, the command to
be given to brigadier Markham, our colonel. Orders were issued
to each regiment as to how they should proceed. My company
was on the inlying picquet. I was orderly corporal, when I
received my orders to take three men, and draw our rations for
the morrow, and get it cooked ready for the morning at three
o'clock. The prisoners were all released; such as those who had
been tried for drunkenness only. All preparations were making
for a bloody day. The quarter-master and his men were busy
getting the ammunition ready, and set a number of camp-followers to dig a large pit, ready for the killed. We quite expected
a warm day's work, and Heaven only knew who had then seen
the sun rise but for the last time. These and many other
thoughts crossed my mind, for we were all expecting a day of
slaughter; and all I wished for was, that the gloomy jaws of the
grave might be deceived of their prey. Then might be seen
the doctor putting his instruments into order, and the attendants
getting ready to carry the wounded and dead away. All these
sights would be sufficient to make a stranger's heart shrink
from the work of death; but I do not think that a thought of
this kind was ever dwelt upon—we were too much intoxicated
with rage at the sight of our dead comrades, and burning to be
at the enemy.

At about three o'clock next morning, we got a dram of grog
each man, and our rations in our haversacks, with hearts swell-
ing for victory. It was about four o'clock, a.m., when we were
all assembled and waiting for the words "go forward." We had got
about the centre of our lines, and halted for further orders from
the General. It was not yet light when we stood in our ranks,
listening to the firing at the outposts, and plainly seeing the
flash from the guns; and who but those who have been in such
a situation can imagine the many thousand thoughts that then
cross the mind? All in one moment it is thinking of home; of

friends dear to the memory ; of things done and now repented of ; that this may be our last day, and hoping we may be happy if this be our last.

We had waited here for a short time, when orders came ; and to our great surprise the order was to counter-march to our camps. This was such a surprise, that it was not easily told what could be the cause. No one could imagine ; but alas ! our surprise was soon known : two hundred-and-fifty of our allies had deserted during the night, and joined the enemy, a number more being expected to follow them. This was nothing more than we suspected ; for Mr. Blacky can never be depended upon. He likes to be on the strongest side. Our whole camp appeared to be panic-struck, and what was to be done then ? I think no one knew ; but there was a great deal of galloping about among our head men. Officers were sent to see what other treachery was going on. They reported that all was well so far ; but unless the enemy were dislodged from their position before night, the whole of our allies would join them, and turn upon us. It was agreed at last that we should fight at once, let what would be the end of it ; and accordingly orders were given to prepare. When the order came, it was about 7 o'clock, a.m., and the news was received with satisfaction.

We assembled in the centre of our lines, composed of the following troops : two troops of horse artillery ; four squadrons of cavalry ; three companies of sappers (with scaling ladders) ; the 1st brigade of infantry ; the 8th, 10th and 52nd regiments native infantry, 2nd brigade ; the 32nd regiment and 51st and 49th regiments native infantry ; the whole not amounting to 6000 men. One regiment, (the 72nd native infantry) were left to guard the camp, with two companies from each regiment, and the foot artillery : while our allies were to divert and draw the enemy's attention by false attacks in front, we were to take circuit to the rear. All was now ready for moving off.

The morning was fine, not a cloud appeared in the sky, and

the sun shone beautifully; and never did it send forth its bright
rays on a prouder little army. We were eager for the combat,
and we felt as though we were sure of victory. Our accoutrements and bright bayonets glistened in the sun, and must have
appeared grand, even to our enemies; but how soon were those
glittering bayonets to be stained with human blood!

We marched in open columns of company, right in front,
ready to wheel into line at any moment; and our brigadier's plan
of battle was to get well round their rear, and make his attack
from that quarter; as he well knew it would be almost impossible
to dislodge them by making the attack in front, their front being
so strong by nature as well as by numbers, and that if we did do
so, our loss must be great. As we were turning their flank,
they directed the whole of their guns upon us; but their balls
fell short at first, on our left; though they soon got our range,
and then several balls came through our ranks, or between the
companies. However, they hurt no one. As soon as they
saw they had got our range, they served their guns as fast as
possible; but our commander (as knowing as they) ordered us
to double march until we had got clear of their balls, which fell
fast. Some of them struck the ground where it was hard, and
bounded over us. The enemy appeared not to be aware of our
intentions, as they let us get round without making any opposition, except a few random cannon shots. I think they fancied
we should never attempt to attack them in their positions.
When we had got far enough round, we wheeled into line and
halted, whilst our brigadier and general took out their telescopes,
and viewed their position. We got upon some sand-hills, and
could see all their movements. They were a large body of
cavalry, formed up in front, and large masses of infantry, moving
about as if now aware of our intentions. They soon commenced
to send out a cloud of skirmishers and mounted videttes. One
of our men said he thought there would be plenty of shooting,
for there was plenty of game in front.

The ground we had to advance over was very irregular, being covered with bushes and sand-hills. On the left was a large, dry, water course, and on the right a large tope of trees; and above these, at a distance, might be seen the tops of the domes in the fort. Our cavalry was ordered to the right flank, and the horse artillery to the front of the line, but more to the left. After our brigadier had taken his observations, he ordered the whole to take ground to the right. This done, he commanded them to advance, each regiment sending out its own skirmishers, to cover its own front; when they and the enemy's commenced to exchange shots as we advanced; but the enemy's skirmishers soon withdrew, and ours were ordered in. We advanced at a very quick pace, and the cannon shot came very fast; though they always fell rather short, and bounded over us. Then, as we advanced, we got under their range, and their balls went over us; so that they had always to be altering their elevations. One ball only took effect, killing one man and wounding another. The enemy's cavalry was now turning our right flank in large bodies, but our little band of cavalry (for they were nothing to the enemy's) were ordered to charge; and charge they did, in a most masterly manner, driving them out of the field towards the walls of the fort. Then, wheeling to the left, they swept up the front at full speed, cutting all down before them. They even cut down some of the artillerymen at their guns. This charge was headed and led by a gallant young officer, the adjutant of one of the irregular regiments of native cavalry. He displayed great courage, sweeping all down before him. As soon as our front was clear, the artillery galloped three or four hundred yards forwards, and poured in a most destructive fire of grape and canister. As soon as we came up to our guns they limbered up, and now came our turn for a charge. At this time, the enemy's balls were flying very thick. I heard them singing about our heads; but strange to say, they did us no hurt. The whole of them appeared to skim above our heads. We were now within three hundred yards of the enemy's line and batteries, when we received the word "charge!" We gave three cheers, and with levelled bayonets into them we rushed. Nothing can be a grander sight than to see a field of victory carried at the point of the British bayonet.

We drove them before us upon their own guns and works, bayoneting the artillerymen at their posts. They were as good soldiers as ever took the field. They would not leave their guns; and when the bayonet was through them they threw their arms round the guns and kissed them, and died. We spiked their pieces as we got possession of them. We drove their infantry into the dry canal, which led to the fort. We stood upon the bank and shot them like ducks; for they had got into such confusion, in trying to make their escape, that they could not move along—they were in one another's road; and the best of it was they could neither return us a shot, nor could they escape out of the canal, the banks on both sides being so steep. It was fairly choked up with dead; all the cannon they had brought into the field were taken, except one. All the horses and ammunition, bullocks and camels, fell into our hands, and all other kinds of stores. We pulled down their batteries, collected the guns and property, and sent them into our camp.

I had a very narrow escape of my life. As I and my comrade were standing upon the bank, one of the enemy lay concealed behind a bush, on the slope of the opposite bank; when he fired at me. The ball went close by my left temple, cutting the bit of hair off and filling my eyes with powder and smoke. I did not know whether I was shot or not, for a short time. I put my hand up to feel. Neither could I see; but my foe was shot in a moment by a sepoy serjeant, and said "very good." As I was not killed, I thought so, too. If he had been still, he very likely would never have been seen.

Another man was picked out of some loose sand. He was covered all over entirely. A great number of deserted allies

N

were amongst the dead. We collected all the dead in heaps,
·and burnt them. This gave our allies a lesson; for they saw
their dead comrades lie amongst the enemy. It was about
eleven o'clock when all was in our possession.

I then thought Moolraj would let us alone for a while. One
of his chief officers was among the wounded. He was a very
large man. He was commander-in-chief of artillery. His
name was Hurry Sing.

It was about three o'clock p.m., when we returned to camp,
and all the men that were left to guard it came out to meet us,
with the band, which played us into camp; while the men
cheered us. Our allies did not know what to do for us; they
jumped, clapped their hands, danced, tapped us on the shoulders, fetched us water to drink, and everything. Our General
ordered us a double allowance of grog and rations.

The next day our brigadier gave us a treat. Our loss was
a mere nothing. Of my regiment one was killed and one
wounded, and the whole loss of killed and wounded did not
amount to fifty men; but that of our enemy was very great.
The name of this action was *Soorujkroond*. The number of
guns taken was seven. On one was an inscription, in the
Persian language. They were all fine brass pieces. The
inscription was as follows, and the Hindoo year when this
action was fought :—

"This gun was made by Futtah Mahomed of Lahore, pupil of Ahamed Yar,
son of the great instructor, by order of the Kalsagee Runjeet Sing, high in power
in the province of Mooltan, with a thousand contrivances, who am named
Nursingham, the cloud-tearer, and aim at the heads of my enemies arrows like
forks of lightning. By the assistance of the superior skill of Ahamed Yar, I
came forth like burning fire; and in the Hindoo year, 1878, I was ready for the
destruction of my enemies."

[The Hindoo year above-mentioned corresponds with our
1821, three years after Mooltan was taken by Runjeet Sing,
January 19th, 1819.]

Copy of a letter from the Commander-in-chief.

Letter No. 490, Camp Tassar, 1848. From the Adjutant General of the army to Major General Whish, C. B., commanding Mooltan field force.

"SIR,—I have the honour, by direction of the Right Honourable the Commander-in-chief, to acknowledge the receipt of your despatch, No 759, of the 7th inst., recording the particulars of an entire, successful, and most spirited attack made by a portion of your force on a strong position taken up by the enemy in front of Lieut. Edwardes' camp; and to assure you that his excellency has derived the greatest satisfaction from hearing of your success, and also from your report of the admirable conduct of the whole of the troops engaged on the morning of the seventh instant.

"Lord Gough desires me to offer his most hearty congratulations on your well merited success; and he requests that you will take the earliest opportunity of making known publicly, to the officers and troops, the expression of his lordship's thanks and acknowledgments, for the very important services they performed in driving the enemy from the intrenched position they had the boldness to take up, at so short a distance in front of the British position. I have much pleasure in inclosing a letter of general orders, issued under the commander-in-chief's instructions, to the army of the Punjab, this day, announcing your brilliant success, and I am directed to state that his excellency cannot otherwise than anticipate the happiest effect from the result of this spirited attack."

"General orders to the army of the Punjab. Head quarters, camp Kispore, 10th November, 1848. The right honourable the Commander-in-chief has this day received intelligence from Major General Whish, C. B., commanding the 1st division of the army of the Punjab, at Mooltan, of an ably-planned and brilliantly-executed attack, made by a portion of the troops under the major generals, commanded by Brigadier General Markham, on the 7th instant, from a strong intrenched position, which the enemy in great force had taken up, within a short distance of the British camp. The enemy was completely routed, with a loss of many hundreds killed ; and seven out of the eight guns he had brought into the field were captured by our troops. The conduct of all ranks engaged on the occasion is described to have been most meritorious ; and while offering to Major General Whish, C. B., and the officers and men under his command, the tribute of his best thanks, his Excellency desires to congratulate the army of the Punjab on the gallant achievements of their comrades at Mooltan."

CHAPTER XI.

AFTER our successful action, we were allowed to enjoy ourselves peaceably and there was great rejoicing in the whole camp. It changed the spirits of both men and officers, and our poor sickly men, who could scarcely crawl before, then appeared to be well all at once.

Hurry Sing died on the 8th of November, of his wounds. He stated, before he died, that Agnew and Anderson were murdered at Mooltan. His body was sent to the enemy, carried by some of the prisoners we had taken, who were liberated for that purpose. Moolraj sent a letter back, accusing Major Edwardes of treacherously murdering two of his officers, who were taken prisoners by the troops; but the accusation was false. He stated that he would surrender on conditions; but no conditions were granted. His letter bore date the Hindoo year, Cuttack 25th, Sumhut 1905; Christian, Nov. 8th, year 1848.

Our men were very unwell now, and a great many died from the bowel complaint, brought on by bad rations, insufficient food, and the damp falling at night.

Nothng extraordinary occurred for a few days. We had supplies brought into our camp by the natives. We could buy rice, fruits, and a little flour, and our communication by our rear was safe. We enjoyed perfect peace among our enemies.

Two of the 72nd regiment of native infantry were getting wood, on the 27th, and went too far to the front, and were taken prisoners by the enemy. They belonged to the band of the 72nd regiment of native infantry. Our horse and foot racing (begun on the 14th) was kept up every other day.

A squadron of cavalry marched out on the morning of the 28th, *en route* to Ballhpoor, to meet and escort the treasury to camp. Our men were still dying fast, but the enemy gave us no trouble.

On the 30th a detachment of men arrived, about 700 strong, composed of men of the different regiments (native and European). They were left, at the time we took the field, in hospital. Most of the native soldiers were men who had been on furlough. The whole were in good health; but a sad misfortune befel one of the apothecaries accompanying the detachment. It appears he had got more drink than he ought to have done, and stopped behind the men, when about seven miles from our camp, and he went in the wrong direction and fell into the hands of the enemy. His body was found by one of our patrols, stripped of all his clothes, cut and hacked all over, and a bullet wound through the head.

We received news of a battle having been fought between Sheer Sing and the commander-in-chief at Ramnuggur. The enemy was compelled to retreat. Our army lost : killed, 1 officer and 14 men; wounded, 9 officers and 54 men; missing, 1 officer and 11 men ; total, 11 officers and 79 men. A royal salute of twenty-one guns was fired from our camp, in honour of the victory. This action was fought on the 22nd of the month.

We had a great deal of drunkenness among our men, which is always so disgraceful to the British army in every country. Although the natives were under a heavy penalty for selling liquor to the men, and some were flogged for it, yet the money was so enticing that they ran the risk, and smuggled it in, in all the craftiest ways imaginable. Our daily allowance was quite sufficient.

On the 5th of December, two of our men were tried by a court martial, and received one hundred lashes for being drunk on duty. These were the first who had been flogged after colonel Brooks was promoted. Two of our officers (captain Moor and lieutenant Richardson) walked a match of five miles, dressed in private soldier's clothes, and in marching order, with knapsack filled with a soldier's kitt, and a musket and 60 rounds of ball cartridge.

One wing of each regiment, with part of the artillery and cavalry, went out on the morning of the 6th, at 4 o'clock, as a reconnoitring party, and to see if the enemy had made any fresh works. We marched to the south side of the city and fort. Lieutenant Edwardes, with a portion of our allies under his command, and a squadron of our cavalry attached, proceeded to the east side. We met with no opposition until we got so near to the walls as to see the men at the guns. They then opened fire, but their balls were very harmless : they did us no hurt. When we had got far enough we halted in the ruins of some gardens, walled all round, which had been very tastefully laid out. There were some fine houses and noble mosques, deserted. They served us for shelter from the enemy's balls, which came whizzing among us rather fast ; but the only effect they took was upon the walls. While we were halted here, I sat under the ruins of some old buildings, and the cannon were loudly roaring from the fort, and the balls were carrying away the branches of the trees) or burying themselves in the sand. I thought, while there, of the horrors of war, and what desolation was around. Those fine buildings and splendid gardens, only a few months before, were in their grandeur, but now the site was a wilderness. There were some fine groups of palm trees and other kinds of fruit, standing in quantities. A little ground was still cultivated by a few natives, in the hope that the contending armies would not come in that quarter again. We had a little mercy upon them, for we kept off their ground as much as possible. They were terrified at us, and hid themselves as much as they could, but I do not think these natives, were more afraid of us than our own men—I mean those who

joined us the day or two before. They had never been under
fire. It amused us to see them duck down their heads, when a
ball came whizzing over us, or shy at one when it struck the
ground near us.

When our General had taken his observations, we returned to
camp, where we arrived about 11 o'clock, a.m. Our enemy
did not follow us; so that we came at our leisure, but covered
with sand, for the sand rose in a cloud as we marched along.
The party that proceeded to the east side captured a convoy of
corn belonging to the enemy. There were forty camels loaded
with it. Our cavalry and the enemy's cavalry escorting it had
a sharp skirmish; but the latter were beaten off with loss, and
their convoy brought to our camp. Sickness still continued
among us; three more men died from dysentery on the 6th.

We had a little rain on the day following, the first we had
after our arrival at Mooltan. The weather became very cold at
night, and as hot during the day. The thermometer stood at
35 degrees in the former, and 90 in the latter. The cold in this
country is not like the cold in England: for it goes through
every vein, and through the whole frame. It brings on the
bowel complaint.

The General received dispatches from the Commander-in-
chief, recording a victory gained by him over Sheer Sing, at
Sundoolapoor, on the 3rd of the month, and effected the
passage of the Chenab. The loss on our side was; in killed,
21 men; wounded, 4 officers and 47 men; missing, 1 man.
Total, 4 officers and 69 men. A royal salute of twenty-one
guns was fired in honour of the victory.

On the 10th, Sheik Mohammed, a native officer under Edwardes, took a portion of his troops and marched up the river
Ravee, to cut off supplies from entering the fort on that side.
He fell in with a small mud fort, on the bank of the river,
occupied by a portion of the enemy. He attacked them
and took it, driving the enemy into the city. They found a

large quantity of stores in the place, belonging originally to the
4th regiment of native infantry, and 11th regiment of native
infantry (Bombay). There was a mystery about these stores :
they were taken from our army in or about 1840, at the time
the British army was engaged in the war in Cabul and Affghanistan. The stores consisted of new clothing and officer's trunks,
boxes and portmanteaus, with uniform and all other kinds
of clothing ; but the latter was very much moth-eaten and
otherwise destroyed.

The 1st division of the Bombay army arrived on the 11th.
It consisted of one troop of horse artillery (9-pounders) and
500 cavalry of the Scinde horse, and the 3rd regiment of Bombay native infantry. They all looked well and in good condition ; but they had long been looked for.

The bandsmen of the 72nd regiment of native infantry made
their escape from the enemy on the 12th. These were the
men who were taken by the enemy on the 27th of the previous
month, when getting wood. After they were taken they enlisted into the Mooltan service, and so made their escape on
the first opportunity. They said that Moolraj encouraged his
men by telling them that the English would have to leave soon,
for that they could not get any reinforcements. They reported
that Mooltan was very strong, and the Mooltanese did not believe we could take it.

We reconnoitred the enemy's position again on the 13th.
Next day, four armed steamers arrived from Bombay. They
took up their stations in the river, to cut off all communication
in that direction, and prevent supplies from entering the fort.
They were but small, but they were well armed and well
manned. All our sick and wounded went to the river on the
16th. They were to go in boats to Ferozepore.

Our cavalry and the enemy's had a sharp encounter on the
18th. The enemy left thirty men on the field, and we four,
with a few horses on both sides. Our cavalry was continually

o

patrolling round the fort, to cut off supplies from going to the enemy, and all their communication with other forces.

The camp colourmen of the Bombay army arrived next day; and the whole army was expected the day after.

Two of the enemy's buglers deserted them on the 20th. They came and gave themselves up before daylight, to the out-lying picquet of the 72nd regiment, native infantry. They were two fine-looking young men. They gave information to the General. They said that Moolraj had heard of our rein- forcements joining us, and that his men were getting very dis- heartened, but that he did all in his power to encourage them.

On the morning of the 21st, the whole of the Bombay army came in. Our band went out to play them into camp. Some of our bandsmen said they should play a tune they had made about them, which they called, " Oh, but you're long a-com- ing." They marched into camp about eight o'clock, a.m., composed of the following regiments: Europeans, 1st Bombay regiment, East India Company, H.M. 60th rifles, one troop of horse artillery, and two companies of foot artillery; native cavalry, 1st regiment of Bombay lancers, with about 1000 Scinde horse:—native infantry, 3rd regiment, 4th regiment native rifles, and 9th and 19th regiments, with native horse and foot artillery. They brought a good park of artillery—70 guns of all sorts. The men all looked well, and were in good health; the whole were under the command of brigadier Dundas. The entire British army now amounted to about 15,000.

We now learnt the cause of the Bombay force being so long upon the way. It appears, when they were ordered to take the field and march for Mooltan, General Auchmuty was in com- mand, and, being the senior of General Whish, he wanted to be chief of the army at Mooltan; but the Commander- in-chief not thinking it proper to take the office away from our General (as he had commenced the siege), this caused General Auchmuty to be very jealous. He is therefore supposed to have made the troops halt at every place he could, and as long as he could, with all kinds of excuses. At one place he delayed them a week, on pretence that they wanted cattle to carry the stores; another time, that the men were all sick; and at another, that the cattle were knocked up. He was sent back under arrest, and the command given to brigadier Dundas, colonel of the 60th rifles; but instead of being tried and cashiered, he was allowed to get off with a reprimand. He ought to have had the severest punishment; for, through his conduct, hundreds of lives were lost, and very nearly the whole of the army; and our sufferings were unknown, from want of provisions.

The enemy fired a salute in the night of the 22nd, from the walls of the fort. They kept up such a fire for about an hour, that it quite illuminated the city. We learnt the cause of it by night. The Dewan, to deceive his men, told them that he had just received news from Sheer Sing, that he had defeated Lord Gough, and was then on his march to their assistance; and to confirm this, he ordered a salute to be fired. It was understood this news was brought by one of our spies. They had had news of our reinforcements joining us, so the Dewan did this to encourage his men. We had orders to change camp, but they were afterwards countermanded, as the artillery part of the Bombay army was not ready.

On Christmas-day we struck our camp, and commenced the march about eight o'clock in the morning. We went to the east side of the fort, and pitched our camp on very nearly the same ground as that we left on the 16th of September, when we gave up the siege and retreated. The enemy kept a very close watch after us all the time. We could see them in large bodies on our left. The country all round this side had a very different appearance. Now, almost all the bush-wood and a great many of the trees were cut down. The two villages, which we left in ruins, and many other buildings, had entirely disappeared. The large sand-hill was made much lower. The enemy had done this, thinking to do harm to us, as we should not have those places for cover; but I thought it had made it much better, for we could see better up to the walls of the town, and over the ground we should have to go across.

The place where Colonel Pottoun and Quartermaster Taylor of my regiment, and a major of the 10th, were buried, was under a tree, close to the left of my regiment. The grave was disturbed, and we thought that the enemy had taken the bodies up; but we opened the grave, and found they had not been removed. Let it be remembered, they were killed on the 12th of September.

The Bombay army removed camp on the 26th, and took up a position on our left. The whole army was now encamped in line, with our right to the north, and our left to the south, and our front to the city. Our allied troops were stationed more to the west of the city, to cut off all supplies, and prevent the enemy from making their escape. We had now taken up our position for the last time, until the place was captured. We could see the enemy's troops in our front; they were in large bodies, and watching us very closely. They appeared very busy throwing up intrenchments.

We received orders on the morning of the 27th, to get our rations cooked, and be ready to take the field by eleven o'clock, p.m.; for the purpose of gaining all the enemy's out-posts, and the suburbs of the town, and driving the enemy within the walls. This was to be the day for the commencement of the final destruction of Mooltan, and its illustrious fortress. All was bustle in our camp, in getting ready. Various orders were received as to what each regiment should do, and what part of the action they should take. All were prepared and eager for the attack. The enemy, on their part, were not idle, as they closely watched every movement they could see along the front of our position.

CHAPTER XII.

THE ATTACK UPON THE SUBURBS.

In the dead of the night the whole army was under arms, and formed up in four columns of attack, in front of our camp and opposite to the enemy's position. As soon as the latter saw us assemble, they suspected what was about to take place; they fired a signal-gun, which was soon answered by one from the fort, and they began to assemble in force to receive us. At half-past twelve o'clock all was reported ready, and moved off to the attack. Three companies of my regiment were ordered to extend, and advance in skirmishing order. As soon as the enemy thought they had got us within range, they opened a furious cannonade upon us; but their balls did little or no harm, although they fell fast. They must have elevated their guns badly, or they certainly must have done us a great deal of harm. When we reached their intrenchments, they commenced a fearful fire of musketry; but this was received with a hearty cheer by our men, who rushed forward and dislodged them from all their advanced works, driving them from post to post. Our horse artillery were not inactive; for wherever an opportunity presented itself, they galloped forward, and gave the enemy a round or two of grape and canister, until they were stopped by the intrenchments, which they could not cross over until roads were cut for that purpose. The enemy were followed up; and as they were driven from one post, they occupied another, which they did not give up without obstinate resistance and desperate fighting. At one place in particular (the large sand-hill) they held out stoutly, disputing every inch of ground. This hill commands the town, and they knew well we should plant our guns upon it; and they so far succeeded as to drive our men back. The hill was very steep, and we were very much out of breath, and the enemy occupied it with such a force, that we were greatly overmatched. The fighting was obstinate; we did not retreat until our major (Case) ordered the bugle to sound "the retreat," as he saw it was impossible for us to take the hill. He took us about four or five hundred yards to the rear, and formed us up again in line (for we were very much out of order before), and he then said, "Come, my lads, we must have it—it must be carried at the point of the bayonet." He then placed himself at our head, and gave the words "forward—charge!" and "charge" we did, never firing a shot until we got close into them, when every shot fetched a man down; but the fighting was awful for a few minutes. The enemy were determined not to give up the hill, and they beat us half down again. However, we soon regained it, and proceeded up the hill inch by inch, and at length gained the crest of it; though they opened such a heavy fire, that our gallant major fell severely wounded, when cheering on his men, with a number of them at the same time. The hill was covered with the enemy's dead, but they gave way, and it was ours. We held our caps upon the top of our bayonets, and gave a hearty good cheer, then driving the enemy before us.

At this time the left or Bombay division came down, carrying all before them, taking the flying enemy in flank, and helping them on a little faster. The first brigade was carrying all before them, and the enemy were driven entirely within the walls; not a man was left alive without, with the exception of two hundred prisoners.

This was all done by five o'clock, and to the great satisfaction of our General. The loss of my regiment was very small, being in killed, one sergeant and one man,—wounded, two officers and nineteen men; but some of these died after. The loss of the whole army amounted to about fifty.

I will here allude to what happened to one of our men; he received three musket shots at the same time. One struck him in the left hand, carrying away the top of the thumb, and cutting all the guides of the fingers through; another struck him in the right hand, in the fleshy part, near the wrist; and another through the fleshy part of the back.

After driving the enemy in, our army commenced throwing up batteries and making intrenchments, as near to the walls as they could. The wall was very high, and full of loop-holes to fire through, which they made good use of. They kept up a continual fire of cannon, and a regular roll of musketry. Our men worked hard all night to get the guns and mortars into battery, ready to open fire at daybreak.

Early on the morning of the 28th, we had a number of guns mounted on the battery; but the enemy kept up a troublesome fire all night, and several artillerymen were shot. As soon as day dawned, so that we could see the walls, our batteries opened fire: salvo after salvo went thundering into the town, both of shot and shell, and must have committed awful destruction. Our guns were within five hundred yards of the walls, and we had possession of some buildings within one hundred yards of the Delhi Gate, where our men and the enemy's kept up a regular fire at each other, wherever any one on either side showed himself. The firing was kept up on both sides very fiercely all day, and our guns dismounted some of the enemy's.

Six young officers now joined us from England. I did not know what they thought of it; but it was rather a rough trial for a new beginner. They soon had to try their maiden steel; one of them was ordered on duty at the intrenchments, with his company, at dark in the evening.

All night the firing on both sides was kept up, quite illuminating all round; while shot and shell were thundering into the town dreadfully, killing men, women, and children. We got more guns into play during the night, and approached much

nearer the walls.   Two breaches were commenced in them, one
at the Delhi Gate, and the other more to the left.   Our guns
were kept in full play all day, and regular rolls of musketry
discharged.   A great many prisoners were taken in trying to
make their escape from the town; but numbers were women
and children.   They were all treated well.

I was now very bad, having had the fever and ague; but I
felt as discontented as I was unwell, for I wanted to be out and
with my company, or they would be saying I was in hospital
while they were fighting.   I did see some men who ought to
be doing their duty, instead of being in the hospital.   When
the doctor came, they were ill, but as soon as he was gone,
they were well enough.   He had to completely drive them out
of hospital, and tell them they were the "Queen's bad bargains;"
and their comrades were always at them, calling them
" schemers."

Whether the enemy were becoming short of shot or not, I
did not know; but they now commenced firing large round
stones.   They threw them from mortars; some of them came
very near our camp.

The firing on both sides was maintained at a gentle, regular
pace, on the morning of the 30th; but at day-break our guns
opened a terrible discharge—salvo after salvo went roaring into
the town, and at the walls.   It was reported that the wall at
the breaches looked very shattered, and that our shot had done
much damage.   At about eight o'clock a shell from one of our
mortars dropped upon one of the enemy's largest magazines
and exploded, when the building blew up with the most terrific
effect ever witnessed.   The fragments were thrown up for a
thousand feet, or more, into the air.   The clouds of smoke,
dust, stones, bricks, mortar, and bodies (for hundreds of people
were employed in the place making up cartridge) were immense.
It is calculated that 800,000 pounds of powder were in the
magazine.   The most fearful devastation was caused by this

occurrence. The Dewan's mother, with several of his relations, and many officers, besides numbers of his troops and people, were blown up into the sky; whilst mosques, domes, houses, and huge masses of masonry came tumbling down in destructive confusion. After the first surprise was over, the effect of this explosion was hailed with the greatest delight by the besieging army. The man who fired the mortar was rewarded with a gold moor. A mighty conflagration was next seen, supposed to be that of the principal store, containing £50,000 worth of grain. The enemy's artillery slackened, but it was still unsilenced; for they opened fire again with redoubled fury. The shock was felt for miles round—it came with such a crash that I thought the ground would open; and the sight was such that I could not give a proper description. It was something like a very large tree shooting forth its branches at once in all directions.—At night a breach was reported at the Delhi gate.

On Sunday (the 31st) the firing on our side was rather slack during the first part of the night, and the enemy's continued about the same; but at twelve o'clock our artillery opened fiercer than ever it was before. This was done to fire the "old year out" and the "new" one "in." The thunder from our batteries was still dreadful: salvo after salvo was fired without ceasing. As many as twenty shells were in the air at the same time, all making their course to the devoted city.

On the first morning of the new year (1849) the firing was continued upon both sides at a regular pace. I got away from the hospital, but was far from well, though more contented in mind. My comrades were all glad to see me amongst them once more.

The cannonade was kept up all night, and shell was thrown into the town—sometimes every minute, and sometimes every ten minutes. The firing from our batteries was fearful, and must have shattered the wall very much. It was reported to the General, in the morning, to be very much damaged, and the

F

breaches to be practicable. Our heavy shot had made good
work; they had battered the wall down in six days. The
enemy made an attack upon our allies, from the south-west
gate, in hope of cutting their way through; but they were
beaten back with loss. A large fire broke out in the fort.
What the cause was, we could not make out: some thought
they were burning their dead, and some, that our shell had
set something in flames. About ten o'clock we received
orders to get our rations cooked, and put in our haver·
sacks. At one o'clock we paraded for the purpose of storming
the city. We moved off to the sandhill, where we halted,
waiting for the Bombay division to come up. We took cover
from the enemy's shot behind the hill, but they kept up a sharp
fire, and several large shot dropped among us. The ground
being very sandy, they buried themselves in it; and numbers
came cutting the wind just above our heads. The hill stood
our friend. As soon as the Bombay division came we were told
off to the breaches we were to storm, and to the part we were
to take in getting into the town. My division consisted of
Her Majesty's 32nd regiment and the 72nd and 49th regiments
of native infantry, and were to storm the Delhi gate. We had a
portion of sappers and pioneers, with scaling ladders attached
to each division. The Bombay division was composed of the
1st Bombay Europeans, East India Company, and two regiments
of native infantry, and were to storm the left breach, or Bohur
gate.

All now being reported ready, we moved off to the breaches;
and as we marched along the enemy appeared to be fully aware
of our intentions, for they directed every piece they could bring
to bear upon us. We moved on sharply, as much as possible
under cover of some buildings; as there were a great many
large buildings and mud huts; so that the only damage they did
was to knock some bricks from the buildings, which flew
amongst us. When my division arrived at their post, we

halted within three hundred yards of the breach, under cover of the buildings as much as we could; and each regiment and company was then told off to what part they should perform— the whole under the command of Brigadier Markham. The grenadiers' company and two battalion companies were to lead, and be the storming party, and the sappers and pioneers were to be directly in their rear, with the scaling ladders. My company, with the remainder, was to support them, and follow up immediately, and direct a good fire upon the enemy, where they showed themselves from the wall or at the breach. We waited at our post ten minutes, or more, and the enemy's balls came clashing among the buildings very fast, and wherever they got sight of us there would come a shower of bullets.

CHAPTER XIII.

THE STORMING.

It was three o'clock in the morning when the bugle sounded "the advance," and the three leading companies rushed forward at the breach, well led on by as brave an officer as ever drew a sword. This was Captain Smith, of the grenadier company, and he was well followed up by the remainder, cheering all the time so loudly that not even the roaring of the guns could be heard, nor the whizzing of the balls. As soon as the storming party charged up to the breach, nothing could be seen but a regular mass of flames pouring from the walls upon us, cutting the branches from the trees, and knocking down pieces of wall, whilst fragments of bricks came dashing among us, cutting and bruising many of the men. I saw ten or twelve knocked down at once by them! The storming party had by this time got up to the walls; and God only knows how to describe the scene here; for no breach was to be found, not even large enough for two men to enter abreast, and our scaling-ladders would scarcely reach them. It was therefore impossible to enter by means of them. The enemy defended the breach to the utmost of their power: they stood with drawn swords at the top, while others kept up a regular fire, and large stones, bricks, with beams of timber, were hurled from the summit of the walls upon us; and even women could be seen loading the muskets for the men, and handing them to them. After Captain Smith had made several attempts to gain a footing, he saw that he had not the least possible chance, only keeping us exposed to the fire of the enemy. He called out "retreat," "get under cover," "there is no breach." But a retreat was not so easily made, for all the rear of the reserve had pressed forward, too eager to take a part in the affair as soon as the leading companies had entered; and we never thought of a retreat. So, before the reserve could get back, or even before they knew what was the matter in front, the leading companies were upon them, thus all became a confused mass, rushing back for cover. Before we could gain cover, however, I saw one of our buglers shot dead, close by me, but a little to my left. The ball struck him in the back, and he reeled round and fell; he was but a youth, not more than eighteen years of age. I saw Captain Smith with the blood streaming from his head; he had been struck with a brick at the breach. Our loss was, in killed, 1 corporal; 2 privates, and 1 bugler; wounded, 2 captains, 1 lieutenant, and one sergeant (mortally), and 19 men. Total, 27.

This was in my regiment. The discontent and confusion rose higher amongst our men on this occasion than on any before; they swore vengeance on the engineer officer who had reported the breach ready, and several of our officers were heard to express themselves in very high terms, Captain Smith in particular. But we did not give ourselves much time for considering. We wheeled to our left, and went at full speed to the left breach. When we arrived there the Bombay division had just entered. They met with little or no opposition; for we had made the first attack at the Delhi gate, and so had drawn the enemy's attention to defend it, and in so doing they had weakened the left breach. We entered the city at once, and spread ourselves all over it in every direction, driving the enemy from street to street, and from square to square, and from house to house. In some places they fought very hard; for they occupied the houses and poured a very heavy fire from the windows and down from the house tops. We broke open the doors with the butt ends of our muskets, and blew off the locks, when not one of those within was left alive: every one being killed on the spot. They were despatched wholesale. One

place was fought very hard for by the enemy. This was a
Hindoo mosque, and was occupied by a brave officer and a
number of determined men. They had a colour, a very handsome one. They were attacked by a party of our men, who
took the colour and killed nearly all the men. The officer
carrying the colour, fought with it in one hand, and his sword
in the other, cheering on his men at the same time; but they
were met by men equally as determined as they. The chief
part of the struggle took place in the mosque, and we were
confined for room : our muskets with the bayonets fixed on the
top we found rather awkward, as we had not room to turn
them about. A man by the name of McGuire, a corporal, was
attacked by the officer bearing the colour: he came sword in
hand, and the corporal not being loaded at the time (for he had
just fired) had quite as much as he could do to defend himself.
However, he parried off the cuts of the sword until he had a
chance, when he made a thrust and gave the officer the
bayonet, and, at the same time, received a cut from the sword
upon the left arm. They closed upon each other, and grappled
each other by the throat; when the corporal gave him the foot
and threw him upon the floor. The corporal then took his
opponent's sword and cut off his head, and brought the colour
away as his prize; but he had received a very large wound upon
his arm, extending from the wrist to the inside of the elbow.

As the enemy retreated, we followed up, driving them before
us down every street or passage, wherever they could be found,
until every one who could make his escape into the fort did
so, and by dark-hour the town was fully in our possession.

I shall here notice the bravery of Lieutenant L. Mansell, of
my regiment, who was attacked in a passage by three of the
enemy. He faced them, sword in hand, and parried off every
one of the cuts that was made at him by the three men; when
one of them made a very heavy cut at him with all his might.
The Lieutenant, in parrying off this, broke off his sword at the

hilt. Luckily for him, some of our men were coming up to his assistance, seeing the encounter, when they fired and killed all three, and never hurt him. The balls went on both sides of him.

To describe the many different horrible scenes which were witnessed, while the fighting was going on in the city, is more than I can do; but I shall try to remember a little. As our fire was poured down the street into the enemy, and they were falling in numbers, intermingled with the men might be seen women and children. Their wild, terrified screams, were awful. The cries of the affrighted children, as they clung round their mothers, were equally dreadful. Grey-headed old men, with their venerable beards white with age, and their flesh deeply furrowed with the wrinkles of seventy or eighty years, whose tottering limbs stood trembling, overwhelmed by grief and age, unable to follow their families, were weeping for the ruin of their country, and lay down to die near the houses where they were born. The streets, the public squares, and especially the mosques, were crowded with these unhappy persons, who mourned as they lay on the remains of their property, with every sign of despair. The victors and the vanquished were now become equally brutish; the former by excess of fortune, the latter by excess of misery. Every one was plundered whom our men could lay their hands upon, regardless of their pitiful cry, and in some instances were women and children shot down amongst the men. Our men now appeared to be brutish beyond everything, having but little mercy for one another—still less for an enemy; and very little pity indeed could be found in any one.

The enemy now being driven into the fort, the town was entirely in our possession. Hundreds lay dead in every direction, and numbers of prisoners were taken. We marched over heaps of dead bodies as we began to collect ourselves together; for regiment had become mixed with regiment, and brigade with brigade. I, with about thirty others, had got along with a native regiment, and could not for some time make out where our regiment was, and when we did find it, half the men had not joined.

Our first act was to collect all the inhabitants together; and to do this we had no small task, as they had entirely built the windows and doors of their houses up with brick and stone, for the purpose of keeping out the pieces of shell which were continually flying about. We had to pull them down, and then break open the doors, and enter, when we were sure to find a number of men, women, and children, terrified and squatted in a corner. We brought them out and escorted them to the middle of the town, or some other place, in order to keep them altogether out of the road, and prevent them giving any information to the enemy. In one of these places which we broke into, there were five women and a number of children, and two or three old men with hollow cheeks and sunken eyes. They looked the picture of misery. I told them not to be afraid, and the women declared that they had had nothing to eat since the siege commenced; for the shell was continually exploding and killing them, if ever they stirred out. I felt very sorry for them, and having a cake and a piece of bread in my haversack, I gave them the bread, saving the cake for myself. They devoured it as greedily as dogs. Had this been at any other time they would not have touched it—not even with their hands; as they consider everything we eat unclean. Some of this work was attended with horrible brutality by our men, which I am almost ashamed to mention. No one with Christian feeling ought to be guilty of such cowardly, unsoldier-like actions, as some of those committed. Englishmen! blush at your cruelty, and be ashamed of the unmanly actions perpetrated upon old men, entirely harmless; and, still worse, upon the poor, helpless women. In several instances, on breaking into the retreats of these unfortunate creatures, a volley of shots was fired amongst them, as they were huddled together in a corner, regardless of old men, women, and children. All shared the same fate. One of my fellow-corporals, who never was worthy of the jacket he wore, was guilty of cold-blooded murder. He shot a poor, grey-headed old man, while he was begging that he would spare, and not hurt, his wife and daughters; nor take away the little property they possessed, consisting of a few paltry silver rings, upon their fingers and in their ears. The fellow pulled the rings off in the most brutal manner. He did not wear his stripes long after; but most of these poor creatures were plundered of every thing they possessed, that was of any value; and what could not be carried away was completely destroyed. I learned that several of the men of our army were guilty of murder, beside the corporal I have mentioned. Our native soldiers were much worse, and more brutish; but they were more to be excused, as they were natives.

I shall here make mention of another crime, more horrible, perhaps, than murder, which tarnishes the glory of British arms— I mean the ravishments committed by some of the soldiers. One of these I know of, and can speak to the truth of the statement. A man of the 3rd company of my regiment, an Irish Roman Catholic, named B——, went into a room, and took a young girl from her mother's side, and perpetrated the offence; for which he has to answer before the God who heard that poor girl's cries and petitions. Had I been upon the spot at the time, I would have shot him dead. When I learnt the fact, I made a vow between God and myself, that if ever I saw any man in the act of committing that horrible deed, I would put a ball through his heart; for many as are the dreadful sights I have seen, that made the blood run chill in my veins.

Some might ask, where were the officers, as they did not put a stop to these things? I answer, three officers to 100

Q

men could not see every thing, and some of them were equally as brutal as the men; and if a complaint was made, it was paid but little attention to amid such circumstances.

Night had now set in, and the town was clear of every armed enemy. We were ordered to different parts, to take possession, and guard against attempts to regain the place. My regiment was ordered to take possession of the Delhi gate, and to occupy the four main streets which led to it. My company occupied the Delhi gate and grand square. We had the Brigadier and most of the staff with us. We piled our arms after planting sentries in all the passages and entries, which were required for our safety. One of our men was very near being killed, as he was on duty, by an old woman. She knew to some powder under ground, and took a piece of cotton which she had got burning, and blew up the place. She intended killing a number of our men; but they had just gone away. The explosion blew her all to pieces: she got that for her pains. It was what she deserved, for she had been well treated.

Our first act was to forage for something to eat, of which we stood in great need. We soon found plenty of cooking utensils, of every description, except knives and forks; these not being used in this country. We found abundance of flour, and butter, and spice of every kind: sugar and salt were also abundant; and in a yard close by we found some buffalo cows, which we milked. We also shot a bullock and a good fat goat; but to skin them we did not wait. We had two large frying pans, and made a fire of doors and windows, or anything we could tear down from the houses. We fried meat and baked cakes, which we made a good meal of, until every one had had sufficient. This done, we dragged the dead bodies out of the square, for it was covered with them. We then found some mats, and spread them upon the ground; they served for beds, and some of the men had dead bodies for pillows.

At about 12 o'clock the moon was shining very clearly, when
I and one of our men went to look for Major Inglis's horse, as
he had left it outside the city before we stormed ; and getting
outside the wall, amongst some old buildings, we heard a
very mournful cry. For some time we could not make out
where it came from ; but at length we found in a solitary hut an
old man. We asked him what was the matter; when he told
us that all he had was gone ; his house, and every-thing he possessed, was burnt, and every soul of his family killed, and he
had nothing to eat, so he had come there to die. All we could
do was to pity him and leave him; and, as we proceeded,
we could see troops of jackalls and dogs, dragging and tearing
the bodies to pieces, and growling as we drove them away.
We came back by the left breach, and so along the inside
of the wall of the city, upon the ramparts, which were covered
with hundreds of the enemy's dead ; and on coming up to
a party of sepoys, we found they had made a large fire of
wood, and in this, to our horror, we saw one of the enemy !
They were burning the poor fellow alive ! They had his
legs in the fire as far as the middle. His cries and groans
were awful. He had been wounded by a musket-shot.
I went and found the native officer, and told him if he did
not shoot the poor fellow, and put him out of his misery,
I should report his conduct to the Brigadier. He said he
did not know of the man being burnt—his party had done
it without his knowledge. They shot the suffering man
at once.

The enemy kept up a steady fire all night, from the fort,
and our mortar batteries continued sending a few shells.
They all came over us as they took their flight into the fort.
The only thing remarkable during the night, was one of
our patrols firing into the other, in mistake for the enemy.
One man was killed, and one wounded. Our loss altogether,
in taking the place, was 350, killed and wounded. As day-

light broke, we could see the breach at the Delhi gate, which we had stormed, and it was well examined. No blame could be attached to the engineer officer for reporting it practicable, for, from the place where he stood to make his observations, it did look so. The distance between him and the wall was at least 400 yards, and he could not see that the ground near the wall fell into a regular trench, ten or twelve feet deep in the centre, a small mud wall running along the top, which parted the road and the ditch. This was about three or four feet high; so that while our batteries had been playing at the bottom of the wall as they supposed, they had been aiming at a part not more than half-way down; and at the distance the batteries were away it did look as if the ground were level. The left breach was a very good one. The ground went with a gradual slope up to it, and a whole company could enter in in line. The discontent was very great in my brigade, for we ought to have stormed the other breach. Our artillery had made it, and the Bombay artillery had been at this.

As daylight dawned on the morning of the third, our men spread themselves all over the town, in search of plunder. All the houses were ransacked, and what could not be carried off was completely destroyed. Temples were broken into, and the brass idols and Korans carried away and sold. I brought some of the brass images or idols away from one temple, intending to keep them as a curiosity, but I gave them away afterwards. Some of our men met with plenty of silk and cloth: swords, matchlocks, muskets, a number of flint guns, and bows and arrows were found, with loads of powder and ball. Some were made up into cartridges, and some were loose in boxes. There were bullets of all sizes. Stables full of horses and harness, and yards full of cattle, camels, and elephants were discovered, the animals being taken by the prize agent and his men. All our men, European and native, looked for the precious metals. They took the rings and chains from every dead man, as well as the living. All that I brought away from the place was a breast-plate, which I took from one of the enemy who was shot when we were storming the town. He belonged to the 6th Kalsagee regiment. I also had a dagger, of the sort which the natives use in close quarters, and a piece of beautiful carpet. This kind of work and destruction was put an end to, as soon as it got to the General's and Brigadier's knowledge; and not before it was time—for every place was turned upside down. After this order was given, many of the men were not satisfied; they took themselves off, and were not checked until several had been sent to camp as prisoners, and one of my regiment was tried and flogged for his conduct.

In describing the town, I may say that the walls are from twenty to thirty feet high, full of loop-holes; and at distances of every 200 yards there are half-moon batteries, every corner and gate being also well flanked with bastions. The inside has a good rampart all round, and is well banked up with earth. They threw up an intrenchment after the siege commenced, to strengthen the wall, and for cover for themselves, and to make the entrance more difficult for us. The streets are very dirty and narrow. The houses are high, and some of them well built, and very tastefully laid out, the wood-work and doors being beautifully carved, and the walls of the rooms (in the higher class houses) covered with splendid paper. What a thousand shames that such splendour should be destroyed! But so it was:—not even a single house or building did I see but what was damaged more or less, as shells had gone through them in some part or other; while thousands of houses were nothing but heaps of ruins—not even a wall was standing whole, and under these might be seen numbers of bodies buried. Heaven only can tell what were the sufferings of those poor creatures after the siege commenced; and no one can ever tell how many were killed. No respect was paid to the nobility of blood, to the innocency of youth, or to the tears of beauty. As we explored the different parts of the town, a death-like silence reigned in the forsaken quarters; the most intrepid were intimidated by the loneliness. Some of the streets were so long, that we could not recognize each other at the opposite extremities—uncertain whether we were friends or enemies, we advanced towards each other cautiously. Mountains of dead lay in every part of the town, and heaps of human ashes in every square, where the bodies had been burnt as they were killed. Some were only half consumed, and were so black that it was almost impossible to tell what the materials were. Many had been gnawed and pulled to pieces by dogs; and arms, legs, heads, and other parts of the corpses lay in every place. The dead horses and beasts which lay about caused a horrid stench, and the town swarmed with millions of flies.

The remainder of our army was at work erecting batteries, and making intrenchments for the siege of the fort. The enemy had taken all their valuables, such as money, jewellery, and the greater part of the silk, into the fort with them. We took a few guns from the enemy.

Thus ends the taking of the city of Mooltan.

CHAPTER XIV.

The reserve of our army having been at work all night, making fresh batteries to play upon the fort, they had brought many guns into play by daylight on the 4th, and these maintained a continual roaring of cannon. The enemy were not idle on their part; for they returned our shot very regularly. They fired a few shells, but they threw a great many large stones from mortars. We heard that the merchants of the town had offered £30,000 to our General not to plunder or meddle with the city any further; but how true it was I did not know, as the most valuable property had been taken to the fort for safety. We were hard at work all day at our intrenchments, and the firing was most deafening. My head felt quite bewildered from the continual roaring of our guns.

If the Sabbath was thought any thing about, when it fell on the 7th of January, in 1849, I think it was observed by a fire fiercer than ever from our batteries. During the night the enemy had got more guns into play, which they opened fire from at daybreak; but they were speedily capsized by our artillery men, who appeared to put their shot wherever they thought proper. We still continued our work at night, in making fresh intrenchments.

On Monday, after working hard all night, we had run our intrenchments within 500 yards of the south angle of the fort, and got a good battery into play at the north angle. The enemy kept up a regular fire from the walls, and wherever any of our men were seen over the bank of our intrenchment, there was sure to be a shower of musket-shot descend on them. We

had several killed and wounded.   Most of the inhabitants were
at large now, and began to put the houses into repair again.
They looked wofully wretched.   Our camp swarmed with
beggars: they would eat anything, caste or no caste, though
a few months before they would not have done so on any
account.   They would eat our unclean food (as they called it)
and were glad to get it.   An officer joined us from England on
this day.   I do not know what he thought of it; but to hear
the continual roaring of cannon and rattle of small arms, must
have been rather terrifying.   He appeared in good spirits.

Our enemy appeared to be gathering strength; for their fire
was continued fiercer than it ever was before.   Their guns
were well served and quickly fired: they kept up a regular roll
of musketry.   They threw a number of shells on Tuesday; but
our artillery were determined to outdo them.   They then threw
shrapnel shell into their batteries, which upset their guns and
killed the men at their posts, compelling their fire to slacken
towards night.   We had several men killed and wounded.   Our
artillery threw more shell than anything else during the night,
and we could hear their wounded groaning after our shells had
exploded, when they had fallen into the fort.   The night was
very still, and during the time our fire had slackened, we could
hear them talking, and their sentinels challenging their reliefs,
as they went their rounds.   We could hear one of the sentinels,
upon the ramparts nearest us, singing, and he appeared quite
happy, as he passed up and down on his post.   We heard him
call out as one of our shells was fired.   This was, I supposed,
to give the alarm to his comrades.   We could hear them strike
the hour upon their "gurrey," and their drums beat and
bugles sound.   Every thing appeared to be going on very
regularly.   We were extending our intrenchments during the
night.

The night having been rather darker than usual on Tuesday,
we took advantage of it, and worked very hard.   We ran our

intrenchments up within less than fifteen yards of the hedge of
the trench surrounding the wall of the fort. I do not
think we were more than twenty yards from the walls. Our
enemy must have thought we were getting very bold, now that
we had got close up to the wall. We had lost several more
men, killed and wounded, and I have not the least doubt that
we should have lost a great many more, had it not been for our
mortar batteries, which threw the shell with such skill as to
fall just within the wall of the fort. This kept them in check.
Some of the pieces from our own shells flew amongst us, and
over us, as they exploded upon the walls. We could now plainly
hear the cries of the wounded and dying; but the besieged
appeared determined to hold out. We could hear their réveille
beat in the morning, and their bugles sounding. On Thursday
our sappers commenced to run a mine under the bank of the
trench, surrounding the fort, so as to blow it in, and fill up the
trench across to the fort-wall, where the breach was begun, and
to give our artillery a better opportunity to get at the wall,
which was very strong and high. Our shot made but very
little progress. There was a large dome, just opposite the
breach, which our shot and shell did great damage to, having
knocked a hole through the top. They did not like our coming
so near, and appeared to wish us to keep at a more respectful
distance; and to punish us for our near approach, they took
the advantage of the night (which was very dark) and made a
sally from one of their sallyports. They attacked one of our
batteries with great spirit, and took one of our working parties
by surprise, who made their escape by leaving their tools
behind them, and getting into the main intrenchments; but
the enemy were beat back in a most gallant style, leaving a
great many dead upon the banks of the intrenchments. We
lost a number in killed and wounded, on this occasion. Our
working party said this surprise was entirely owing to the 4th
regiment of Bombay native rifles, their covering party, who,

R

when the enemy attacked them, retired without firing a shot, leaving them at work. Some of them said that they, in making their escape, ran through the enemy, and were not noticed amid the confusion and darkness. I believe that some of our men were killed and wounded by our own shots; for it was so dark that we could not distinguish one party from another. It is said that a number of the enemy made their escape, and went off. The attack took place about 11 o'clock, p.m. The firing on both sides was kept up all night; so that the fort all round was in a continual blaze.

On the 12th we made a very large battery in the city, to play upon the fort from this side, which opened with a most thundering fire. The distance between the fort and city is, I think, as near as I can say, four or five hundred yards, and had been used as a parade ground for their troops. It had a long range of stabling and sheds round it, and it was truly awful to see the poor horses and cattle there, dying from hunger. They ate pieces of leather and cloth, and even gnawed the wood through. Their misery was dreadful. We shot some of them for pity's sake; they were very good horses, and some of them had their harness upon them. We dared not fetch them out, nor dared the enemy; for if we made an attempt they fired upon us, and if they did we fired upon them. There were also a number of the enemy lying dead amongst them. The town smelt very bad from the number of dead lying about, gnawed and dragged about the streets. Some I saw half buried and half above ground. What a sight for the inhabitants, to see their fellow-townsmen lie scattered about in all parts of the town, and most likely their sons, brothers, or fathers, or some near relatives! I thought of my own dear country, and hoped that such a sight might never be seen there.

The firing was kept up very regularly on Saturday the 13th. Our engineer officers took up their quarters in Moolraj's palace (as our men call it). They went there to be nearer their work.

This place had been occupied by our troops, as one of our advance posts; but it stood rather back, and was not in immediate danger, although they pitched a shot at it some times, or threw a large stone, which had struck it in several places. It was a very handsome place. It had a wall all round, and a large square yard, with buildings, or dwellings, very beautifully painted. On the walls were figured plants of different kinds, and trees, and various animals, and most of the wood-work was carved. The yard was laid out in very fine style, and was very clean. In another yard were tanks of water and baths. It was the finest place I saw in this part of the country. I was informed that it was where the Dewan Moolraj kept his wives and his concubines.—We had rain all day, which made everything very uncomfortable. We had not a dry thread upon us by night, and we stood up to our knees in mud. We were now worn out with fatigue and want of rest, and the general feeling was, that they wished the enemy would surrender, or an end be put to the affair in some way or other.

Much rain fell during the night, and it was very cold. Our intrenchments were all of a slough. In spite of the rain, our fire was still kept up, but that of the enemy slackened; for most of their guns were dismounted by our shot. In the morning our enemy commenced a new plan of fighting: they filled earthen pots with powder, and put a fusee to them, and threw them at us from the fort; and they got bladders and leather bags, and did the same with them. They did this to try to burn us, but they did us no harm, as we could get out of their way. After they had tried this for a while, they gave it up; there were not many of them reached our trenches. They were determined to annoy us as much as possible; so as they could not do any good with their first plan, they commenced to throw bricks and stones at us. Out of the ditch of the fort we could hear them say, in their tongue, as they threw them, "English pigs." This caused a little merriment in our trenches.

We picked them up, and threw them back again. We were not more than fifteen or twenty yards from each other, and as our officers began to suspect that they were running a mine under us from the ditch of the fort, we were ordered to throw in hand grenades—small shells about the size of a cricket ball. This was to clear the ditch of them; for when the grenades exploded, they would kill wherever they hit. They were some time before they were driven out, and some of the grenades, which had not exploded, they threw back at us. The wall looked very much beaten, and large pieces of masonry had begun to fall; but there were three walls, one higher than the other. The first wall was all we wanted to make a breach through.

The firing was slack all night, and the weather took up; but as soon as daylight broke on the fifteenth, our guns opened their fire. Shot and shell were sent into the fort, and salvo after salvo, at a fearful rate; and the roll of musketry was still kept up. All our men looked very bad: we were nothing more than like bags of bones.

On the next day the enemy got several guns into play, but they were speedily dismounted by the superior skill of our artillery. The enemy threw a number of inferior shells, which were not very destructive. We had a few men killed and wounded. While two of our companies were relieving outposts in the morning, the enemy opened a fire of musketry upon them, and Captain Bryan fell, very severely wounded by a musket ball through the small of the back. His life was in great danger for a length of time. He was a fine-looking, brave officer; but he will always be a cripple. There was great sorrow at this misfortune, through the whole regiment; for he was very much respected by the men. The enemy were deserting whenever they had an opportunity to escape from the fort: they were fired on by us, or by the enemy themselves, and so were killed. I believe if we had not fired upon them, a great many would have deserted, as the fort must have been getting too hot for them. The smell from the dead was very bad : it was sufficient to create a plague in our camp. The troops of jackalls, which were always prowling about at night, were getting quite fat with their feast of human flesh ; the vultures and ravens were also growing too lazy to fly away as we passed them, while they were sitting upon and pecking the bodies of the dead.

Our firing was still kept up very briskly on the 17th. As day broke, about two hundred of the enemy came out of the fort, to give themselves up to us ; and as we did not know their intentions, we fired into them, when about fifty of them fell killed and wounded, before we knew what their intentions were. We sent them prisoners to Lieut. Edwardes' camp. They said that a great number more would desert if we did not fire upon them. It was now clear that our shell and shot were making the fort too hot for them. They stated that our shell had committed dreadful destruction, and that the fort was in an awful state.

The news brought by the prisoners gave our men fresh courage, the shot and shell being afterwards sent in at a most murderous rate. The enemy never could live amid such a terrible fire. About 11 o'clock at night, and under cover of darkness (for it was very dark), the enemy made a desperate attempt to cut their way through our lines, and make their escape from the fort ; but they were steadily repulsed. They fought with wonderful courage, but they were opposed by men whose courage never was surpassed by that of any other nation. They were driven back, leaving many dead behind them.

Our shell and shot were fired at a most fearful rate all night on the 18th, and the walls began to look an entire mass of ruins. The breach had crumbled very much. Most of their guns were silenced, and the fort must have been in a dreadful state. We sprang a mine opposite to the breach, but it did not fill the ditch up sufficient for us to cross—it was so deep.

The firing on our side was still kept up at a murderous rate on the 20th. I felt for the garrison in their situation ; for they were brave men and very determined still to hold out. The place now looked like an entire heap of ruins. The walls on our side were crumbling fast before the weight of our heavy shot. Another mine was sprung to blow in the counterscarp of the ditch. We heard that we were to storm next day, and I hoped the news was true ; as we had been long enough at it to wear out the strongest màn, and our men were all anxious to be at them.

The firing from our batteries into the fort was maintained at a fiercer pace than ever, and the roll of musketry was kept up all night. The more ruinous the fort looked, the more courage our men had. One of our bravest officers was wounded on the 21st, by the explosion of one of the enemy's shells : he received a very severe wound across the back of the shoulder. His name was Maunsell—the young officer who is mentioned before for his brave defence of himself against three of the enemy at the storming.

The enemy sent out an officer bearing a flag of truce. He proposed to surrender. The officer was conducted to the General, and was kindly treated ; but what took place between them we did not know. We were given to understand that the Moolraj wanted to surrender. Our General let him know that he might do so, but it must be unconditionally. The officer was then conducted back to the fort.

The firing was kept up all day on the 21st at a regular pace. The Moolraj sent out another flag of truce in the evening, with a message, stating that he would surrender at sunrise on the morning of the 22nd. It was plain that they were now beat out. The news was received with much satisfaction by all. Orders were given in the evening that we were to prepare ourselves to take the fort in the morning, either by surrender or storm. If the enemy failed to surrender at the proposed time, we were to storm, and orders were given to that effect. The storming party was told off, and the remainder received instructions accordingly.

The whole army assembled in the morning at 4 o'clock, for the purpose of storming the fort, or receiving the enemy on surrender. We left a strong guard in camp; and before we had been assembled five minutes we had not a dry thread upon us, the rain falling in torrents, and the ground being a regular sheet of water. We were obliged to reverse our arms to keep them dry, and the water from going down the barrels. We marched off at the time appointed, and took up our positions; but it was not yet light. We were stationed in the intrenchments, as near to the fort as we could get. My regiment was to storm, and we were as near to the breach as possible, and in front of our batteries, which were playing over us. The trenches were up to our knees in water and slough, and the rain still fell heavily. The reserve was better sheltered : they had taken up their positions in the temples and buildings, a little to the rear. In this plight we waited for the appointed time to surrender, or the signal to storm. We waited for an hour or more, and the rain still fell as fast as ever; but in spite of that, our batteries kept up a regular, steady fire, and a straggling roll of musketry might be heard. The firing on the part of the enemy was but feeble, whether of cannon or musketry. Many were the reports that ran through our ranks while waiting here. Some said the enemy would not surrender, because they had not seen the sun rise; and others, that we were to storm. Our men were greatly out of patience, and wished the General would let us go forward. For my part, I wished so too ; for I was tired of standing there up to my knees in water, and the rain still falling. Still it was a good thing we did not storm; as many lives were spared which would otherwise have been lost. Our men, tired with a long siege,

wet, and hungry, swore vengeance against all, and declared
that they would spare no one. At length the enemy began to
come out of the fort by the eastern gate, and an order was sent
round to the batteries to cease firing; but the battery I was
nearest to had just fired a salvo, when the orderly arrived with
the order, and the officer in command got upon the trail of one
of the guns, to see if the shot was taking proper effect, when a
ball from the walls of the fort struck him in the breast, and he
fell dead. This was the last man killed at Mooltan, and he was
taken and buried under the flag staff in the fort. This was
also the last shot fired at Mooltan on our side; though the
enemy, as if determined to have the last blow—perhaps more
from treachery—just as we had all mounted the bank of the
intrenchment, supposing there would be no more firing, discharged a cannon-shot from one of their guns, which just
skimmed over our heads, hurting nobody.

One division of our army was ordered to form a square at the
gate, and as the enemy came out they laid down their arms,
being received as prisoners by us; while the other division
occupied the fort as the enemy withdrew. My company was
ordered to receive the Dewan Moolraj as a prisoner, when he
came out, which we did, and escorted him to camp. One man
took hold of his horse's head, while the company formed on
either side of him. He was accompanied by seven of his officers.
He was dressed all in red, or a crimson silk; his cloak was of
the same kind, very richly embroidered. He had a gold chain
round his neck, and gold bracelets on his wrists, richly set with
stones, and upon his finger he had a diamond ring. He was a
good-looking man, of the middle stature, having fine features
and a mild countenance, yet a keen, piercing eye, and a determined expression. He was altogether a fine, pleasant, good-
humoured looking man. I could not help but feel for him;
indeed, I felt very sorry for him. When we had got about
half way to the camp, he turned round upon his horse, and

viewed the fort, and tears then started from his eyes, and he
wept much; and well he might, to see it then!—battered to a
heap of ruins, while only a few months before it bade defiance
to the British force and the world, and was proud of its strength
and beauty. The Dewan passed many jokes with our men,
and talked frequently to them. His officers were very attentive
to him. He gave his sword up to the officer who was interpre-
ter for him, and the latter delivered it up to the General.

The appearance of the enemy, as they came out, was very
dirty and wretched: they had a number of wounded, whom
they carried out upon cots, borne by four of their comrades
or friends. They were a most determined-looking set of men,
and had even a savage appearance. Most of them were loaded
with property, but they had to leave it at the gate. Amongst
the enemy who came out, was a man of the 10th regiment, who,
it will be remembered, was taken prisoner on the night of the
9th of September, when Colonel Pottoun made an attack
upon the villages. He looked very bad, and had never been
shaved. His wounds were healed, but his arm was crippled,
and part of his toes were amputated from one foot. He had
several other wounds about him. He said he had had the best
of treatment, until of late, when he was neglected; and some
days he got food, and some days he got none. The enemy were
hard pressed, and therefore could not attend to him. The poor
fellow wept for joy as soon as he saw us. A crowd of men
and officers soon collected round him, but his Colonel sent him
off to camp. As soon as the enemy had all come out, they
were marched off to our allied camp, and we saw no more of
them. The last cannon-shot that was fired, was fired by a
number of the Kalsagee artillery, who were not for giving up.
They said that they would rather die at their guns than give
up, and they did not, until the Dewan sent an express order for
them to do so, or they would be fired on, and that it would be
useless to resist.

s

Mooltan, the fort, the garrison, and the Dewan, were now all in our possession. I heard that it was never known for a fort to hold out so long, after the town had been taken, before. The number of men surrendered, I heard, was about 4000; and the number of guns taken in the fort was 54, and 4 mortars—all brass, and some of very large calibre. This made in the whole, taken at Mooltan, about 68 guns of all sorts; but their loss in killed and wounded will never be known. The loss of the British army at Mooltan was—in officers, 13 killed and 51 wounded; and the number of men killed and wounded, 1153; making in the whole, 1217. I should think we lost as many as this by deaths from fatigue and disease, brought on by the hardships we underwent.

The latter part of the day was very fine, and we beheld with glad hearts the British flag proudly waving in the breeze. That flag which has never been subdued by any nation, and which the sun never sets upon, was planted upon the fort of Mooltan; and hard as the struggle was to place it there, it would require a still harder to strike it.

Moolraj was quite free with our men, before we were relieved; and said that we were good soldiers, and that we looked like nothing but beardless boys.

CHAPTER XV.

After a siege of twenty-seven days we got a good night's rest, which refreshed us very much. As for myself, I thought when I awoke that I had not been asleep more than a quarter of an hour, and could not believe my eyes when I saw it was broad daylight. I went and visited the fort on the 23rd, and such a sight I never before saw. Scattered all over the fort lay dead horses, bullocks, camels and men, as thick as they could lie, mangled in all the most horrible ways imaginable, and the smell was quite unbearable. Some lay half devoured by dogs, and others were far advanced in putrefaction. We set the natives to bury and burn them to get rid of the smell. Not one single building stood whole, and more than half were battered to the ground. One of the large temples was an entire heap of ruins, and the other was a very large, strong-built place, but it had received several heavy shocks from the weight of our shell. There were some of their old prophets' tombs in this; yet it was very dirty. They had some very good and well-built magazines.

The destruction all round the one that was blown up was woful; the buildings were nothing but heaps of ruins, one upon another, and some of the corn stores were on fire, having been so ever since the 30th of the preceding month. Some thousands of quarters of corn lay burnt to ashes, and were still burning. They had got plenty of stores, of every description, so that we should have been a long time starving them out. It would have taken us as long as it did Runjeet Sing, when he laid siege to it. I have been told by some that he was seven years, and by others that he was three years, in getting possession.

We found a great deal of our officers' baggage, and mess stores of every description, which had been taken from us by the enemy. The baggage consisted of boxes, trunks, portmanteaus, carpet-bags, and other effects; and many casks of wine and liquors. Our letters were also found, and the letter-bags, which the enemy had taken at the time they took our posts. Some of the letters they had opened, and some they had not. The barracks were very good, but filthy; and had been sharing the fate of the other buildings. The Dewan's palace took share alike with the rest. The treasury was near to Moolraj's house, and all the gold and silver, and precious stones, and money were kept there, in a kind of a cave, under ground. There must have been a large quantity of gold and silver, for it occupied the greater part of three days to weigh, and count, and take away in ammunition wagons. It did not all consist of coin: there were gold and silver bars, and the coin was all of different countries—of Europe, Asia, and America. Some of our men, on duty in the fort all night, came out in the morning loaded with gold. It is said that some of them had as much as £6000 worth of gold; but whether this was true or not I cannot say, though they had a very great deal. However, it never did them any good; for they would give the weight of gold for the weight of grog, which caused a great deal of drunkenness; and as one man got drunk and could not help himself, another would rob him, and *he* would have it until *he* got drunk, and then came *his* turn to be robbed; and so it went on, until the black men got it all for drink. The money was so plentiful that the men would not carry copper; and some of them who had got the most would not carry silver!

I saw all the enemy's guns: some of them were very fine. The superior skill of our artillery had made sad work with them; for I saw three guns with one of our balls stuck in them about half way up the bore, and many had been struck on the edge of the muzzle; and very few of the carriages remained

whole. I saw three or four small guns, which had been struck
by one of our heavy shot, and were broken through the middle.
This showed good practice in our artillery. The situation of
the fort was very high, and had a good command all round; and
how they let us approach with such a little loss is wonderful.
It will never be taken again with such little loss. From the
top of the large dome an army might be seen in motion twelve
miles away. There were three walls; all one within the other,
and all one above the other, and there was a large ditch all
round, from thirty to forty feet in width, and about the same in
depth.

I saw the breach which we were to storm, and I believe that
many lives would have been lost before we should have got in.
It was very steep—steeper than the roof of any house; and the
bricks and mortar and stone which lay about were all loose; so
that it would have been very difficult to have gained a footing.
They had nine guns loaded with grape shot and pice
(a little, thick kind of coin, about the weight of an English
halfpenny). Those nine guns were loaded up to the very
muzzle, and set just opposite the breach; therefore, the first
party which gained the top would have had a sweeping. There
was also a large quantity of opium, all trampled under foot.
A royal salute of twenty-one guns was fired in honour of the
capture of the fort, and thus finished the war at Mooltan.

A royal salute was fired in the evening in honour of a battle
fought by the Commander-in-chief, at Chillianwallah, on the
13th of the month. The Commander-in-chief called it a victory;
but it was dearly bought, by a great loss of life, and four guns.
Half the 24th regiment was cut up, and one of their colours
taken. Two native regiments suffered nearly as badly, with
the loss of their colours. One troop of European artillery was
cut up at the guns. This was caused by a blunder of the 14th
regiment of light dragoons, which behaved in a most cowardly
manner (as was stated by men of other regiments who wrote to

us and wished we were with them, for they wanted no more victory paid for so dearly as that) : they stated that Sheer Sing's troops fought well, but twelve of their guns fell into the hands of our men, so that the enemy gained four and lost twelve.

The General inspected us on the 25th, and gave us great credit for our good conduct, and for our perseverance during a long siege. The inhabitants were now returning to the town; they were all liberated, with the exception of those who bore arms.

On the 26th our Brigadier inspected us, and released two prisoners who had been confined for being drunk on duty. The two officers (Agnew and Anderson) who were murdered here, were found on this day by a servant to one of them, who had been a prisoner in the fort from the date of the murder. The bodies were taken up and buried under the flag-staff, in the fort. All the European bands of each regiment were in attendance, and played the "Dead March," from the place where the officers fell to the fort. They were easily known by their hair being of different colours, although their bodies were far advanced in putrefaction. A ball had passed through one of their heads, and other wounds were quite plain to be seen. We received orders to march in the morning.

My brigade (the 2nd) struck our camp at three o'clock on the morning of the 27th, and marched off about four o'clock. We were accompanied by the band of the 60th rifles, who played us out about two miles. We were composed of the following troops : H.M. 32nd regiment, and 51st and 72nd regiments, native infantry, with one troop of horse artillery, one regiment of native cavalry, and 400 sappers and miners. The General marched with our brigade. We were to make forced marches, and advance upon the town and garrison of Chinout ; and so effect a junction with Lord Gough, as quickly

as possible—the other brigades were to follow in succession.
As we marched, the jungle became very thick; and the 60th
band, which had just been playing "The girl I left behind me,"
turned back, and I thought of the many poor men *I* had left
behind me, and my comrades who lay scattered round Mooltan,
whose bones lay bleaching in the sun. We were in hopes that
when we had taken this place we had done fighting; but not
so—we had to renew the battle again. All the villages as
we passed were in ruins, with no inhabitants except a few old
grey-headed, tottering, men and women. The ground we
marched over, towards the end of the day, was covered with a
thick crust of salt, and the water in the wells was very
brackish. We halted and pitched our camp in the thick
jungle, after a long day's march and in a burning sun. Our
rations were served out, but we were too tired to cook them,
and we had no cooks, they having run away at Mooltan. We
did the best we could with our bread and water. Colonel
Brooks left us this day to go to Bombay, for the purpose of
resuming the duties of his staff appointment.

We struck our camp at an early hour next day, and the jungle
continued densely thick, which made our marching very bad,
as we could not see; and we were frequently stumbling into
the bush, as we wound our way through. We were marching
in a north-easterly direction, by the instruction of our engineer
officers, who took their observations in the same way as it is
done at sea. They went forward with the advanced guard, and
pressed guides to take them from one village to another; and
as they went forward, they marked the way we were to march,
by setting fire to the grass, which burnt in a volume of flames,
and illuminated the country for miles around. When day
broke, they pointed the way by pecking up the earth in places,
or by cutting a bough off the bushes as they passed. We
pitched our camp about nine o'clock. The church prayers
were read in the evening (the day being Sunday) by the Major

(Inglis), who was then in command of the regiment; and a brave man, too, well respected by the whole of the men. He gained their affection on the 12th of September, by his cool and steady conduct, after Colonel Pottoun was killed, when the command fell upon him. He was but a young man; he was promoted just before we took the field. Before that, he was Captain of my company, and was very smart, and was proud of us; and he was a very proper man to command a flank company. We all hoped he might soon be Colonel.

We struck our camp at four o'clock, on the 29th, and as we continued our march we began to pass small patches of corn, looking well. We came to several villages, which appeared to be better inhabited, and began to show that they had not suffered so much from the war.

About ten o'clock we came up to a large village, which had a wall all round, and a small fort in good repair, built of bricks, but it mounted no guns. We pitched our camp beside it, and on the same ground that the enemy had quitted a short time before. They were driven from the place by Sheikh Emaumood-deen, in command of a division of our allied troops from Edwardes' camp. Narain Sing was in command of a division of the enemy from Mooltan. This place was called Sirdar-pore. A quantity of our stores was found here, which had been captured by Narain Sing's division.

We halted here on the 30th, while our engineers and sappers constructed a bridge of boats over the river, to enable our guns and baggage and ourselves to cross. We had been marching with the river a few miles to our left until now. Some of our men robbed the captured stores during the night; they took several bottles of liquors, but they were taken by the picquet. It is a strange thing that some British soldiers will drink so; they would get drunk if they were going to be shot the next minute.

On the last day of January we struck our camp at an early

hour, and marched through some fine corn and cotton fields. We passed several fine topes of trees. At daylight we came up to the river Ravee, and crossed in good order, without any accident, and proceeded on our march. We passed some villages, well inhabited, and the corn-fields looked promising. We pitched our camp about nine o'clock, by the side of a fine village, where the natives appeared industrious, and were tilling their ground.

Our rations were wretchedly bad and dear. We could not buy anything but flour, and not that at any time. We paid three-pence a pound, and that for the coarsest kind. It was nothing more than corn split in three or four parts, and full of chaff and dirt, and even straw an inch long; and it was so coarse that we could not stick it together to make a cake of it. Our chief living was our pound of bread and pound of meat, or rather, skin and bone, and rice boiled; and we had to turn out after our day's march, and cook it under a burning sun. This was through not having good, faithful cooks. Our men felt it bitterly, and often wished that we could fall in with the enemy and kill them at once; or that we might be put out of our misery.

The villagers said the reason why they had got no flour was that Sheer Sing sent foraging parties out to take all the corn and flour they could find; and paid them for none, robbing them in every way.

On the 2nd of February we struck camp, at the usual hour, having had a long day's march. The first part of the day's march was very jungly, but as we drew nearer the end the ground appeared well tilled. We pitched our camp in a fine tope of trees, and close by the side of an old ruin, apparently a fort, which was once of great strength and of good size; but it was entirely demolished, and had been so for a long time. Trees of a large size had grown upon it. The natives said that Alexander the Great laid siege to and demolished it, and that

T

he never went further than this place, for his troops mutinied and would not go any further this way. The town lies about half a-mile east from the old ruins, and was of some size.

On the 3rd we struck our camp at two o'clock, and marched through a dense jungle of thick, strong grass. The stalks were more like wood than grass, and were six or seven inches thick, and from twelve to fourteen feet in height. It was thickly studded with low bushwood, which made it very bad marching; but at daylight we came up to some patches of corn, and we halted about ten o'clock, and pitched our camp. This was a long day's march, and our men were dead beat up from weakness and faintness, owing to want of proper food. Several fainted in the ranks. The General gave us great credit for our exertions, and said that the reason we made such long days' marches was, to effect a junction with the grand army, for the Commander-in-Chief required our assistance.

On Monday, the 5th, we struck our camp, at four o'clock, and marched through a dense jungle, except for the last two miles, when we passed over a country well tilled. We pitched our camp about ten o'clock, near to a large village or town, well built and remarkably clean; but the only inhabitants were old men, and women and children—the able-bodied men being with Sheer Sing, fighting against our army. We could get no provisions, the enemy having plundered all this part of the country.

At the usual hour on the 6th we struck camp, and marched over a large sandy plain, which was so large that when we were in the middle it looked like a sea; for we could not discern a tree or shrub of any kind, and it was quite level, having the appearance of water all round. This was caused by the glimmering of the sun upon the sand, but it was bad to march upon, as it was loose, and at every step our feet slipped back, and the clouds of sand rose so thick that we had great difficulty in breathing.

We passed several patches of corn, at daylight on the 7th, and marched across another sandy plain, and by several small villages. Soon after daylight we came in sight of mountains. This was a long day's march, and numbers of men fell, completely beaten out. I was ordered to fall to the rear, and take charge of the men of my company, and to bring them up as well as I could. Many of them wished they were dead, or had been killed at Mooltan; and I was of the same mind, and began to feel that I would rather die than live in such misery. Several of our baggage camels and cattle, and some of our cavalry horses, dropped dead in the ranks. We halted about ten o'clock, and could not pitch our camp, owing to the camels being knocked up; they had not arrived, and we lay on the burning sand waiting for them; and when they came up we pitched the bell of the tent only—for we were too fatigued to do more; and as for cooking, but little of that was done until night, when the air had grown cooler.

Nine howitzers, which had been sent forward from the brigade in our rear, reached our camp on the 8th; as we expected to come in contact with the enemy on that day. The bullocks drew the gun carriages, and the guns were carried on the backs of elephants; but it tried the strength and courage of both men and beast, as it was more than twenty-six miles to Chunout.

We had scarcely time to snatch a little food, such as it was, early in the morning of the 9th, before our drums beat the "arouse." Weary, faint, and hungry, off we marched; we had not got far before men and beast began to fall to the rear; and before daylight we could hear the booming of the distant guns, as they carried the well-known sound amid the darkness of the morn; but, instead of being an unwelcome sound to our men, it seemed to put a fresh spirit in them. Some of them shouted out joyfully; though many were obliged to yield to weakness, and fainted in the ranks, and would not fall out until they dropped. More than once my head began to swim, and my body trembled all over, and my knees began to bend under me; but by drinking a good draught of water my weakness went off again. As day broke, we passed the ruins of several villages, which plainly shewed that the ravages of savage war had done their work. Numbers of dead bodies also lay scattered around, whose bones were bleached by the sun. The crops, too, were all destroyed: they were either eaten off by the cattle, or trampled underfoot. The wells of water were half full of corpses, which were putrid, and this water we were obliged to drink. We could now hear the firing plainly; but the enemy did not appear to have many guns. About nine o'clock we came in sight of the town, then a good distance off. A range of small mountains runs up to it, and we could see the smoke rise from the guns as they were fired. We halted here for rather more than half an hour, to give time for our sick and baggage to come up, so that we might all be together. After we had halted, all joined the ranks who were able, and we marched off in sections of three, bayonets fixed. This was the plan of our gallant Brigadier; so that as we marched up to the town, we looked like a long string of men, which I have not the least doubt deceived the enemy. They did not fire a shot at us as we marched by the town. We pitched our camp on the east side, about a mile from the wall, about half-past eleven o'clock; but before we had time to get the camp pitched, the enemy sent a flag of truce to say that they should surrender in the morning at sunrise. Still the firing was kept up by Sheikh Emaumood-deen and the enemy. We could plainly see the people in the town, crowded upon the housetops, looking towards our camp; and the sight of us was enough; though I think if they had known our real state, they would not have been afraid, as we could scarcely get up when once down. The firing was not very brisk between our allies and the enemy.

The town is situated upon the plain, at the foot of a small mountain, which commands the whole of the place. It was under the command of Narain Sing, one of Moolraj's chief officers, who was sent out from Mooltan with this force, to bring in supplies and escort convoys to the fort; but by their stopping away too long, we had succeeded in taking all the suburbs, and commencing the siege. To keep him in check, and prevent him from making a junction with Sheer Sing, Sheikh Emaumood-deen was sent from Edwardes' camp in command of a division of our allies to engage him. They had fought two or three severe engagements, and had driven him to take cover in this town.

CHAPTER XVI.

A CANNON was fired at times, and a straggling fire of musketry was heard, on the 9th: but we had had a comfortable
night's rest, which we stood in great need of, and it greatly
refreshed the whole. At day-break we rose, and cooked
our rations, which were very small, and at sunrise we formed
line in front of the town, and as soon as all was reported
ready, we marched in that order upon the town. The natives
were squatted upon the walls and house-tops, to see us as
we advanced. We approached within a few hundred yards
of the walls, and then halted, and formed in order to storm
the town; for so it was to be, if the enemy refused to
surrender. We had no time to spare; so that the town was
to be taken, one way or other, that day. However, after
a short delay, they threw open the gate, and we marched
up to it, and received them prisoners. As they came out
they grounded their arms, and surrendered themselves up.
They were the finest-looking men I had seen, and were armed
in the best style; their arms were all of the first make and
quality, and they were very clean; but they were the most
determined-looking set of fellows I ever saw, and they did
not mind to tell us they never should have given up to a
man of the same colour as themselves. They said they should
not have surrendered to Sheikh Emaumood-deen; but they
added, they thought it of no use to hold out against the
white faces. Narain Sing came out and delivered up his
sword, and told us he never should have surrendered to
our allies; nor should he have surrendered to us without a

blow for it, if he had known our strength, for he could have
held out longer behind those walls. He was a fine-looking
man, with a bold eye, but had a most villainous aspect. He
was very vulgar; he had not the least politeness. He had
about 2000 men, or more, under his command. We took
him with us, but the remainder were left with our allies, who
took possession of the town. The ememy had two brass
guns, and a camel battery of eleven zembaroucks, or guns,
which were fired from the camels' backs, and worked upon
a swivel. The town had a wall all round it, and was flanked
by half-moon batteries at each angle. There was a small
fort on the north side, but it mounted no guns. There
were some fine gardens and topes of trees upon the plain.
On the north-west side was a mountain, which overlooked
the town; and upon this Sheikh Emaumood-deen had planted
his gun to play upon it. He had but one gun; so we left
the guns with him that we had taken from the enemy. We
had several colours given up to us by the enemy; but we
gave them to the General. Two small brass drums, and
one large drum, we kept, with a bugle or two. There
was no property of any value, and the camels and cattle
were given to our allies, who well deserved them. A mounted
orderly arrived at our camp, with dispatches from the Commander-in-chief, for us to push on as fast as possible; as
the enemy were trying to cross the Chenaub river, and intending to march upon Lahore. Our cavalry were to make
the best of their way and join the reserve army at Ramnuggur, for it was short of cavalry. Our cavalry struck
their camp, and marched in the evening about four o'clock,
for Ramnuggur.

We had Narain Sing with us on our march, with our rear-
guard. He had a good horse, and a few servants to attend
him. He was one of the most curious men I ever saw. He
would drink any kind of liquor and get drunk, and he was

full of talk. Some of it was very base and unfit talk. He said we had better not go any further, for he should not like to see such good little soldiers as we were, killed. He compared us to boys, and told us that Sheer Sing would kill us all, and drive every white man out of the country. We marched through some corn fields. This was the finest part of the country we had been in hitherto. We pitched our camp about ten o'clock, a.m. Our officers shot a wild pig in the evening—the first pig I had seen in the Punjaub. They never keep pigs; they do not eat swine. They say pork is unclean, and their religion will not, therefore, allow them to have pigs.

On the day following (Sunday) we passed through a delightful part of the country, The corn and cotton fields looked beautiful. We saw some villages, which were very clean, and the fields all round them were well cultivated with corn, cotton, and vegetables. Topes of trees were studded all round. The country looked more like a garden: as our men said, it was the real Garden of Eden. We pitched our camp at half-past ten o'clock; but not before half our brigade was beaten up. I saw several men weeping, and they would not give up until they fell to the ground, fainting from weakness and fatigue. I only know myself, what I felt several times; I wished that I had been shot; for the marching was worse than the fighting. Some of our allied troops were sent to meet us with flour, but it was not half sufficient—it was soon all sold. We mixed it up with water, and so turning it into dough, and then making a fire of sticks or straw, or anything we could get, we put it on the embers, to get hot through. As for me, I was hungry enough to eat it raw, and it was eaten not more than half done. We had but little time for cooking and but little to cook with. Church prayers were read by the Colonel in the evening.

Weary and weak, we commenced another long day's march at two o'clock on the next morning. The road was very heavy marching, the sand being very thick and loose, and

before we had walked many miles upon our road, men began
to fall in the ranks; and as the sun rose and grew hot,
the sand flew about, and the numbers increased. I was
ordered to fall out and get the men of my company on as
well as I could; but there were but three of them—one by the
name of T. Flinn, was an old soldier, who had been in India
twenty-two years, and who was never beat up before. He
cried like a child, and when we reached our camp, I felt so
sorry for him, that I gave him my grog.

On Tuesday, at daylight, we crossed a very large plain, the
largest I have seen. There was not so much as a tree or shrub
to be seen: nor a blade of grass. There was not a rise nor
hill; but all was as smooth as glass, as far as our eyes could
reach.

About six miles before we got to Ramnuggur, the ground
appeared to be well-cultivated, and several villages began to
appear, scattered around. The country all round was open
and level. We could see the town long before we arrived at
it, and the river, which winds its course along about two miles
from the town. We could also see the British camp, pitched
between the town and the river. It had a beautiful appearance, the white canvass walls shining in the sun, and the tents
being pitched in regular order along the banks.

We marched up to the town about half-past ten o'clock,
and pitched our camp on the east side. The ground all round
was strewn with dead bodies of horses, camels, and bullocks,
which had been killed, or had died from fatigue, and the skeletons of several men were seen.

The Commander-in-chief first came in contact with Shere
Sing on this spot. It was on this plain he fought his first
battle, on the 22nd of Nov., 1848, and at a very short distance
away he forced the passage of the river Chenaub, on the 3rd of
Dec. 1848. The well that we had to draw our water from had
several dead men in; one black man was floating on the top of

U

it, with his face downwards, his body swollen, and twice the natural size. As it was impossible to make use of this water any longer, as it stank so very bad, our water-carriers had to fetch some from a well against the town, a mile away. Before we could pitch our camp, we had to clear away the dead bodies; and the stench was intolerable, as they were all alive with insects, and covered with thousands of flies. The smell of the ground, after they were gone, was awful; but we could get plenty of flour, and everything we wanted, except clothing, and that we stood in great need of, for we could scarcely tell which was the master-piece of our jackets and trowsers. We could buy native-made shirts; but the merchants soon began to take the advantage, and so raised the price of everything. This was the depôt of stores for the army. The town is not large, but it has a brick wall all round.

The reserve army, under the command of Sir Dudley Hill, was on the bank of the river, about a mile from our camp, and guarding the ford, this being the main ford across the river Chenaub, on the road from Cabool to Lahore. It therefore required a strong force to hold it, and to keep open the communication, and take charge of the magazines and stores. The reserve had but one European regiment with it—the 53rd, and there was not the whole of that regiment. Brigadiers General Haverlack and Cureton were killed here, on the 22nd of November. They were two brave and distinguished old officers. As we could obtain plenty of supplies here, we for once enjoyed a good meal, which we had not done for many months. A great number of the wounded arrived here in the evening, from the grand army, on their way to Lahore. Many men of the 24th regiment were amongst them; they said that Shere Sing had struck his camp, and was in full march, but where to they did not know. It was expected that he intended to march upon Lahore. He appeared to be quite a match for Lord Gough. We were ordered to watch the fords, and our cavalry were patrolling the river both ways along the banks for miles, to watch his movements.

We were obliged to shift our camp on Thursday, further from the smell of the putrid bodies, which we could not bear any longer. The 53rd regiment, with some sepoys and cavalry and artillery, marched off at 12 o'clock at night, as news had come that a party of the enemy had been seen crossing the river towards Wuzeerabad. This brigade was ordered to march towards that place. We were to be ready to do so at a moment's notice. Everything was packed up, and ready for loading.

On Friday, our first brigade joined us, about 12 o'clock. It was composed of H.M. 10th regiment, and 8th and 52nd regiments of native infantry, with cavalry. The men were greatly beaten up like ourselves. They were ordered to join us at once, and they had been marching from two o'clock the day before. Who knows the horrors of war but those who are the performers? At about one o'clock, I was in the bazaar, buying some flour and other things for myself and comrade, so that we might have a supply by us, when I heard our bugle sound the "turn-out" for our brigade, and orders were given in haste for us to strike our camp and march immediately. All was now hurry, but in a few minutes we had our camp struck, and our baggage loaded, and every man ready under arms, and we were marched off: but to where, we did not know. We took the direction of Wuzeerabad, keeping the river on our left. We heard, as we were marching, that the enemy's cavalry had been seen on the left bank of the river, as if looking for a ford; and we were to keep them from crossing. We marched over a fine cultivated country, and passed numerous villages. We halted at dark hour, about ten o'clock, and pitched our camp in a field of corn, which was about a foot high. The night was very dark, and we knew not where we were. We were ordered to make no fires, nor have any lights. So, tired and hungry, we pitched our camps, and lay down for the night; but of sleep we had little, as we knew nothing of the enemy, nor the moment they might be upon us. Nor did we know which way we had come—it was so dark; so that we should have stood but a poor chance, if attacked in that situation.

On Saturday, the 17th, we heard that the enemy's main army was not more than nine miles from us. Our artillery and cavalry were encamped near to the river, to watch the ford; and another brigade was at Wuzeerabad, to watch the enemy's movements there, and to prevent them from crossing, and were collecting all the boats they could. Our brigade had orders to do the same. Our engineers were constructing a pontoon bridge, for us to cross as soon as we should be ordered. Mounted orderlies were hourly arriving with despatches, with intelligence of the movements of the enemy. It was now plainly to be seen that a great battle was about to be fought. All the preparations were making, and we were working round the enemy; so that he would be obliged to fight. It was the wish of all of us that it might decide the war. We were in momentary expectation of marching to join Lord Gough.

Next day being Sunday, we had church prayers in the morning, as usual. We had orders to pack up all our baggage, and strike our tents, with the exception of the tops, which we let stand, to keep off the sun, then getting powerful. Our rations were also cooked, and put in our haversacks, slung at our sides. My comrade and I made some flour and water cakes; but we were now put to it for wood to make a fire, for there was no wood about. Some of our men went to the next village to get some, but could not: so they set to work and pulled down the doors and window-shutters, and the natives resisted them. This caused some of our men to strike them; and one poor woman was nearly killed. The men were ordered under confinement for their brutishness; though they had no punishment, as we could not spare men to be in confinement. Every man that was able to carry arms was wanted to fight.

Mounted orderlies were continually coming and going to and from our camp, with despatches. We learned from one that the enemy were about ten miles on the other side the river, and had taken up position in full force at a town called Goojerat; and that Lord Gough was getting round them, and taking up his ground opposite to them. It was now quite clear that this was to be a finishing blow. After waiting all day with our baggage packed, we were ordered to unload the cattle and let them feed, which they did upon the growing corn close to the camp. This was a thousand pities, but it was necessary, for our cattle could not be allowed to be away from us, as we expected to march every moment. We were ordered to cook what rations we had, and our allowance of grog was served out, and we lay upon our arms for the night.

On Monday we were obliged to get wood, with which to cook our rations, from the village, which we completely destroyed, through pulling down the doors and door-frames. The poor natives begged very hard of us to spare them. God help them! I felt very sorry for them, when we had to go into their houses and take away such of their property as we could burn. I thought of my own dear country, and what I should have felt, had it been my case. They cried and begged most pitifully; but such are the horrors of war. The cattle had eaten and trampled underfoot many acres of corn. About one o'clock an orderly came in with a despatch from Lord Gough, with orders for us to march to the river, and cross it at the ford in the evening at dark (so that the enemy should not observe our movements), and to join the grand army in the morning. At three o'clock, p.m., we loaded our baggage upon the cattle, and

marched for the river. The country all round, as far as we
could see, between the river and the village, was cultivated with
sugar-cane. We arrived at the river just as night was setting
in; it was about 400 yards across, with a rapid stream, and
upon the near side was a large head of sand, but the opposite
bank was quite steep, washed by the water as it flowed downwards. Our men forded it; it took them about up to their
arms. Four sick men and I (being orderly corporal) had to get
our baggage across. This was no small task, there being only
a few boats to take across all the baggage belonging to the
brigade. We unloaded the cattle on the sand, and sent them
across. Now the next job was to load the boats; but to
get one was no easy matter, for every one wanted to have the first
turn. It was now all pushing and shoving to secure an empty
boat, as they returned from the opposite side. The native boat-
men not understanding our language, and some shouting to
them in one place and some in another, they were quite bewildered. One or two of them, when they got to the side, gave
us the slip, and, owing to the darkness, we could not see them;
and no wonder at them—for some were cursing at them on one
side, and some on the other. All was confusion. I thought
the best plan would be to sit down until they had all done: I
could not make any rush at one with my weak force, as the
men in charge of the other company's baggage were all stout
men. It was not well planned by our color-sergeant to give
me four sickly men; but I took a second thought, as I did not
see any chance of getting my baggage across. I took one of
my men, and just as a boat was shoving off, we jumped into it,
and went to the other side with it, and when it was unloaded
we brought it back, directing the men where to steer for; so
we got the boat and stuck to it, until we had brought all our
baggage across. It was breaking day before all was taken
over. We met with no accident; but the artillery had an
ammunition wagon in the river. It capsized out of the boat, and

they had a great deal of trouble in lifting it up again. The
brigade piled their arms in line and bivouacked upon the
ground in their wet clothes, for the night, ready to face the
enemy, should they attack us. I never was so beaten up in my
life before, as I was on this occasion; for all the heavy work
fell upon me. My bones ached all over my body, and as we
had now done our work, and had no fresh orders, I lay down
upon the ground, and soon was fast asleep. It rained fast for
half-an-hour; so that I was wet through, but I felt not that,
nor any thing else, until I was awoke by one of our men. I
had lain for an hour-and-a-half, and rose greatly refreshed.

It was now daylight on the 21st. We had a dram of grog
per man, and as we had had nothing to eat since the morning
before, we had a pound of bread per man. Some meat was
killed, but we had neither time to have it served out, nor to
cook it, nor means to cook it with. I was very hungry, and
soon finished my pound loaf, as being the readiest way of carrying it; and I think all the rest did the same. As soon as this
was done, the division marched forward to join the Commander-
in-chief, with a good advance-guard to lead, and leaving about
300 men to load and guard the baggage, and to follow as quickly
as possible, which we did; and before we (the baggage guard)
left the banks of the river, another brigade arrived on the
opposite side—the 53rd regiment and two native regiments with
cavalry and artillery. As soon as they crossed they were to
march up the left bank, to keep the enemy from crossing. We
marched over a fine country, well cultivated with cotton, sugar-
cane, and corn, which were all looking well. Our division
made a junction with Lord Gough's army about 10 o'clock, a.m.
He came to meet us, accompanied by a large body of officers.
He is a fine-looking old man; his head is as white as wool.
He told us he was glad to see us, for he required our assistance.
He said he was surprised to see us look so well, after our
extreme marching and the laborious siege at Mooltan. He

observed that we looked well used to the sun; for our faces
were well sun-baked. He told us we were a set of hardy young
veterans (the regiment all seeming to be young men), and that
we should soon have satisfaction out of Shere Sing for his
treachery at Mooltan.

The men of Lord Gough's army were glad to see us, being
before very low spirited. They told us that they expected the
enemy would attack them every day, for that they were very
superior in number, and were daily receiving fresh reinforcements; that they had become very bold since the battle of
Chillianwallah, where our army got the worst of it; and that
the enemy was quite sure of victory.

It was about three o'clock when we arrived with the baggage,
and we found the whole army had struck camp, taking ground
to the right, so as to let the right flank of our army rest upon
the river Chenaub. We could see the enemy's mounted
videttes along the front, watching our movements. As I kept
along with my baggage we came up to that of the whole army,
and such a mass I never before saw: thousands upon thousands
of camels and elephants and bullocks were all loaded and
moving one way. I heard an officer say, that if they were all
put one behind another, they would reach fifty miles. I took
care to keep on the outside of this mass; for I well knew if we
got in the midst of them, we must go the same way as the rest,
and were sure to get well trampled upon and crushed. Such
a confusion I never before heard—camels bawling, elephants
roaring, and natives jabbering. We could not hear one
another speak. The army took up a position in line, the front
towards the enemy; and the whole line, from flank to flank, was
about five miles long. I found my division pretty early; for I
knew they would take the right of the whole line. It was now
about six o'clock, p.m., and I was so tired and hungry that I
lay down and did not care what became of me. My head was
very bad from the heat of the sun, and I felt quite delirious.

After resting for an hour or two, we got our grog and rations served out, and then pitched our tents in a beautiful field of corn about knee high. This being done, we had orders from the Commander-in-chief to be off duty that night; and a guard of sepoys was sent from another regiment to do our duty in camp. We were all too much knocked up for cooking; one of the men of my tent boiled some rice, but before he brought it we had eaten a bit of bread, and were all fast asleep.

We had orders for a general parade in the morning, and we supposed it was for inspection; but as it afterwards turned out, it was for the Sikhs to inspect us. We had been thirty hours on the march, and thirty-six hours since we had had anything to eat except the pound of bread.

v

CHAPTER XVII.

A LITTLE before four, a.m., on the morning of the 21st, the
orderly sergeant came to call the corporals to go and see the
rations drawn, and get them cooked immediately. This order
had not been given many minutes, before another came, for us
to strike our camp and pack our baggage upon the cattle, as
quickly as possible. This was sufficient to convince us what
kind of parade we were going to have, and was a good sign of
a general fight, too. Our hungry cattle had cropped off the
growing corn close to the ground, for a mile or more all round
the camp. We had just made fires, and got our frying pans on,
and our baggage was not packed, nor the camp struck, when
the well-known sound of the bugle was heard, ringing through
the camp, for us to stand to arms. All now was confusion : we
got a dram of grog served out per man, and a pound of bread
for every two comrades. Our accoutrements were soon upon
us, and muskets in our hands. Some might be seen with a
slice of raw meat in their grasp, which they had snatched up
as they went by; and others were running with their bread in
their hands, eating it as they went. I caught hold of some
meat out of the frying pan, as it was upon the fire, which had
not been on long, so it was raw or nearly so; but I was hungry
enough to eat my boot soles, if it had been possible. I had
often heard talk of a hungry army; but none could be more
hungry than this. We were reduced to nothing but skin and
bone. My bones were ready to come through my skin; and
as some of the men remarked, their ribs would make gridirons;
yet our men were all in high spirits, and appeared eager for

the battle. As the whole army on both sides was here, we determined to make this a finishing stroke. Had the Commander-in-chief only told us there was a good breakfast in the enemy's camp, it would have been all he needed to say. We left our camp and baggage upon the ground, and our cooking utensils on the fire, with no one with them but the tent men, and a small guard to bring them forward.

The whole army was now formed for battle, in a line fronting the enemy, who appeared to be watching us very closely, for we could see them upon every rising ground, and on the tops of the houses at the village. We could discern a great stir in their camp, as if they were preparing to receive us. Horsemen were riding about at full speed, as if to carry orders to the different parts of their position. As we now stood formed for battle, awaiting further orders to advance, I took a survey of the country all round us. It was a level plain, well cultivated, the corn a little above knee high, with here and there a fresh ploughed piece of ground. In our front were topes of trees and numerous small villages, scattered about the plain, which the enemy appeared to make good use of; as we could see them strongly posted in them. The city of Goojerat was visible about four miles in our front. This was the enemy's head-quarters, and the centre of his position, from which he had a good view, and so could watch all our movements.

The morning was fine and clear, and as the sun rose it cast forth its golden rays in great splendour upon the two opposing armies, as they stood with glistening accoutrements, waiting to commence the deadly strife. It was about six o'clock, a.m.. when the line advanced, covered by skirmishers, who soon became engaged with the enemy. They retired, as we came up, out of most of their advanced villages. Our line kept good order, as if on a common parade. The artillery was now ordered forward, and a most fearful cannonading commenced, such as had never been heard before; the whole artillery of both armies being now in full play upon each other. We were ordered to lie down, so that the enemy's shot might pass over us; and over us they did pass, tearing up the ground all round us, until it looked as if it had been fresh ploughed, and we were covered with earth, though not many were killed. The enemy's artillery deserved great credit; for their guns were served in good style, and very regularly. They made some fine shots. Two of our ammunition wagons were blown up by them, and many of our artillery-men killed at their guns; while several of the artillery horses and bullocks were carried away at one shot, and some of our guns disabled. On our side, the shots were thrown in a masterly manner, and shell was pitched very skillfully, killing every man at their guns, blowing up their magazines, and committing woeful havoc. Our shot dismounted their guns, and swept the men away wholesale, leaving them quite helpless.

Our loss was not so great as might have been expected; but I must here mention Captain Anderson, of the Horse Artillery, belonging to my brigade, who had been with us through the whole war, and was as kind-hearted an old gentleman as ever drew sword. His battery was exposed to a heavy cross fire, and he and nearly all of them were killed. He was wounded first by a round shot, and was requested to go to the rear; but he said he would have another shot or two first, when he was struck by another and killed, and his brave men never flinched from their guns, although exposed to such a destructive fire.

The artillery had been in play about two hours, when the enemy's guns began to slacken. We had most of this time been lying down upon the ground, and the enemy's shot had been flying thick about us, and two anxious hours they were; they appeared more like two years, and many were the thoughts that crossed the mind. We got impatient, for all the cry was, "Let us be at them." The infantry was now ordered to advance; and, as we went forward, we could see the enemy forming their line to receive us. They commenced firing at a long range of musketry. We advanced, and did not discharge a shot till within 150 yards or less, when we opened such a murderous and well-directed fire that they fell by hundreds. They, on their part, kept up a good fire, but it was badly directed; as most of their balls went over our heads. They also showed great skill in their movements; for they made a gallant attempt to turn our right flank. To oppose this, our right was thrown back, and the right brigade of cavalry was ordered to charge, which they did in a splendid style, cutting the enemy down in all directions, and driving them back in disorder. By this time, the fight had become general along the whole line: roll after roll of musketry rent the air, and clouds of smoke rose high and thick, while death was dealt out without mercy; and now was heard the well-known shout of " Victory." With levelled bayonets we charged; but they could not stand the shock of cold steel. They gave way in all directions; although some of their officers showed the most daring courage. They tried to rally their men by waving their swords, and going in front of them, to urge them forward; but these brave men were soon shot down, and on we went, clearing the field before us; while all the cry was, " We'll finish them to-day." The enemy formed several squares, to keep us in check, whilst they got their guns away; but our field artillery galloped to the front, and opened a most destructive fire of grape and canister, which swept them down by whole battalions. On we rushed, bearing all down before us, charging and cheering. We took every gun we came up to, but their artillery fought desperately: they stood and defended their guns to the last. They threw their arms round them, kissed them, and died. Others would spit at us, when the bayonet was through their bodies. Some of their struggles were desperate. Some of the guns and carriages were streaming with blood. An aide-de-camp now rode up with orders from Lord Gough, to say that the right of the line was too forward, and that we were to halt. The left now appeared to be getting the worst of it, the villages being thicker and more strongly occupied by the enemy, and every one having to be taken by storm. The East India Company's Bengal native regiment of Europeans suffered severely, as a number of those villages fell in their front; and this regiment deserves the greatest credit for its bravery, for it carried all before it. This was a very trying time for the right of the line. While standing, waiting for orders to advance, the enemy were boldly re-forming their line in our front, and keeping up a fire upon us; although it was nearly harmless, as they (as usual) fired high. Our men were with the greatest difficulty in the world kept in check by the officers. Lord Gough sent a second order for the right to keep back, as the left could not get up; and the brigadier told the aide-de-camp that he could not keep the men back, nor did he, until he rode at all hazard in the front of the line, telling the men to cease firing and to halt. The enemy now had brought some guns to bear upon us with grape. The first round they fired fell just in front of us, and as the ground was fresh ploughed, the shots buried themselves in it; but the second round came, and it fell rather short, slightly wounding one of our men, and severely wounding another. They also made a gap in the 51st regiment of native infantry, which was upon the point of giving way, had it not been for the exertions of the officers, who pressed it to go forward; and I was told that one of the officers cut a man down for refusing. One of the Sikh cavalry regiments, bearing a black flag, then deliberately formed line in front of us, as if about to charge us, when our men could stand it no longer. We opened fire upon them, and whether any word "forward" was given or not, I do not know; but forward we went, and when near to them, and just as they were about to spring forward upon us, we opened such a well-directed fire, and poured it into them with such deadly effect, that it fetched down man and horse by scores to the ground, while numbers of saddles were emptied, and the horses went off leaving their lifeless riders behind.   On we went, charging and cheering, bearing all down before us ; and the black flag fell into our hands, which we bore from the field in triumph.   Everything was carried before us, and the dead and dying lay strewed all over the ground in heaps.   In some places might be seen men lying in whole ranks, as they fell ; and in more than one place I saw artillerymen and horses one upon another, as they had been shot down by whole batteries, at the time their guns were dismounted.   The carriages lay broken and scattered in all directions.   The enemy, as they retreated, made daring attempts to stand at the villages ; but they were stormed, and very few escaped, for they were all either shot or bayonetted. The left of our line suffered the most, the villages lying the thickest in their front.   However, nothing could daunt the courage of the British soldiers, nor resist the shock of the levelled bayonets.   We drove them before us in disorder through their camp, which was pitched round Goojerat.   We captured all their tents and camp equipage, with all their stores and magazines, and nearly all their artillery.

We stormed Goojerat, where all their principal stores and treasure were.   Sheer Sing himself had but a narrow escape : he had been upon a high building, so as to see and direct the battle.   It was reported we had entered the town before he left it.   We came up to one place, where a strong guard was posted over some treasure, and spare arms.   We called on them to surrender, and give up their arms ; but they would not—they said, " No, we will not give up to any English." One of our men was going up to the sentinel, to disarm him, but the sentinel shot him dead on the spot.   One of our officers then told them they had better surrender, as it was useless to resist; and he was going to disarm the sentinel, when he wounded him. We were then obliged to fire into them, and they were nearly all killed before the rest would surrender. The enemy were now driven from the field, and were in full retreat, in the greatest disorder, with nothing left but what they carried. Our cavalry was in full chase after them, cutting them down in all directions; and the ground for miles was strewed with dead. Such a slaughter never before was made. One of our cavalry told me they followed them for upwards of ten miles, sabring them as fast as they came up to them.

Our cavalry continued the chase after the flying enemy until darkness put an end to it. Some of the cavalry did not find their way back until the morning, as the night was so dark.

It was now about four o'clock, p.m., when we halted, and the Commander-in-chief ordered us a dram of grog per man; and we cheered our aged general as he rode along the ranks. Our next thing was to collect the captured guns, stores, horses, elephants, camels and bullocks. We set fire to the camp, and destroyed the powder, the quantity of which was enormous. I never could have believed that they had so much. Tons upon tons were buried in the ground, which we blew up. Lord Gough came amongst us, and was very full of jokes. He said that the enemy's teeth were drawn, and that they were totally defeated.

After we had collected the captured guns and stores, we pitched our camp about two or three miles away; but a great deal of our baggage did not arrive until morning, owing to the darkness. The men had got miles away, another road. I was in charge of my baggage, and was at a great deal of trouble to find my regiment, and my company was outlying picquet. As soon as we got in, we thought of procuring something to eat, having had only one pound and a half of bread since the morning of the 19th, that is, during more than sixty hours.

The loss in my regiment was a mere nothing: we had one man killed, and one officer and five men wounded. The loss of the whole army was, in killed, 5 officers and 91 men; wounded, 24 officers and 682 men, with 5 men missing; making in all, 807.

The battle commenced about six o'clock, a.m., and lasted until darkness put an end to the chase. The loss on our side was wonderfully small in comparison with the enemy's. My regiment captured two colours and a "gurrey," or thing to strike the hour upon. We took a great many prisoners, who told us that Sheer Sing was going to attack us in another day or two, and that he would have driven us into the sea, and killed every white man in the country, but he had not calculated upon the enemy he had to meet; he did not think of the Mooltan force being there, burning for revenge, and determined to have it, for his treachery and desertion at Mooltan.

In this battle, as in all others, the enemy fired very high. Their shots went whizzing over our heads by showers, when they ought to have been doing the greatest execution. The only way I can account for their doing so is, owing to the large quantity of powder which they put in their cartridge, and so, from the overcharge, causing the ball to rise. Some of their cartridges were from four to six inches long, and the balls were not so large nor heavy as our musket balls. The enemy fought well, and showed great skill. On more than one occasion they attempted to outflank us, and repeatedly made rallies to form their line again; but nothing could surpass the skill with which our artillery were served and played upon the enemy wherever they attempted to make a stand. Some of their squares were nearly all carried away by our grape and canister. In the villages the enemy were all put to the bayonet. Not one escaped. All the streets were choked up with the bodies, and every nook and corner was full. Dykes and trenches were equally crammed with dead and dying, and the field all round

W

was covered. It must have been a terrible day for the enemy. I do not know how many guns were taken, but a great many. I think I saw four of ours which we had retaken. These were lost by Lord Gough's army at Chillianwallah. The enemy's guns were very fine. Some of them were very large, and I saw many of the carriages beautifully ornamented with polished steel and ivory, let into the wood-work, in the shapes of animals of different kinds, and of the gods they worship. Their artillery horses were very good, and their harness too; and everything was clean and in good order.

When we asked some of the prisoners if they had had enough of fighting, and if they were tired of it, they said they were not—they should fight again yet; and if we fought fair they could beat us. They asked us what our officers gave us to make us drunk with; for we must be drunk, they said, when we shouted, and ran up to their batteries, in the face of their fire, and to the mouth of their guns. They called us " beardless boys," and said we must be mad, or fools, to go up to their fire in the way we did. They might well call us " beardless boys," for we were about as thin as herrings.

I do not know the native regiments that were engaged in this battle; but the European were, Her Majesty's 10th, 24th, 29th, 32nd, 60th, 61st, and six companies of the 53rd (but they were not engaged). The cavalry regiments were, Her Majesty's 3rd Light Dragoons, 9th Lancers, and 14th Light Dragoons, and one regiment of the East India Company's Bengal Europeans, with a suitable portion of horse and foot artillery. Sheer Sing, with a few of his cavalry, made off towards the river Jullum.

Some of the prisoners told us that if we had not attacked them, they were going to attack us in a few more days; for they were preparing for it, as they knew that Mooltan had fallen, and they intended to make their attack before the Mooltan army joined Lord Gough. They did not know that

we had joined him until they saw us in the field. They had
begun to throw up very extensive field-works. This Lord
Gough knew, and so attacked them before the works had gone
forward enough to be of any service. They were greatly surprised when they knew that we had joined the army. They
did not think that we should have marched from Mooltan so
quickly.

CHAPTER XVIII.

Two divisions of infantry and all the cavalry and horse artillery that could be spared marched in pursuit of the enemy on the 22nd. We spent most of the day in cleaning and cooking. I went round one or two villages, and into a temple, and whereever I went were heaps of dead. We found several wounded, whom we conveyed to our hospital, and we gave them some food, for which they were very thankful.

On the day following we had a very heavy hail-storm. The hail-stones were very large. It was the first I saw in the country. We could discern the mountains of Affghanistan very plainly with the snow upon the tops, from this place.

On the 24th some of the enemy's guns were found in a village which they had abandoned in their flight. Some of our cavalry returned, and said that Sheer Sing was in full flight, with about 1000 cavalry—all that remained of his once grand army. With the exception of these few it had been cut to pieces and dispersed. He crossed the river Jullum with his party, and was in march towards Peshawur. Our cavalry was close after him, and expected to come up with him before he reached the Indus. Never was an army so completely destroyed before.

On Sunday, the 26th, the smell from the dead was so bad that we were obliged to shift our camp, for fear of getting a plague amongst us. We marched about four miles away. A sad accident happened after we had pitched our camp: some of the lascars and artillerymen were arranging the ammunition wagons, when one of them blew up, killing one European artilleryman and five natives, and wounding a number more.

A portion of our army was ordered to march towards
Peshawur, on the 2nd of March, in charge of a siege train.
They were to join General Gilbert, then in pursuit of the
enemy.

On Saturday, the 3rd, the Commander-in-chief inspected the
whole of the troops. He was in fine spirits, and looked well.

A number of prisoners came in on the morning of the 5th,
under escort of the 11th native cavalry. We heard that Sheer
Sing was taken. It appears that he had got as far as the river
Indus, and wanted to cross; but the few men he had would not
go with him, being wearied out and heart-broken. Our advance
guard got up to them the same night; so he and his few men
surrendered to General Gilbert. Lord Gough gave a dinner to
all the field officers at night, and the men did well too, getting
plenty to eat: they did not feel like the same men.

The captured guns were sent down the country on the 6th,
under an escort of cavalry and infantry.

The day after, an order was given that no man was to go to
the city, on account of a fever breaking out—no doubt owing
to the bad smell of the numbers of putrid bodies which lay
around the place.

Our heavy artillery marched on the morning of the 11th,
towards Ramnuggur. This we thought was a very good sign
that we were going to have no more fighting.

On the 12th, we changed our camp about six miles to the
rear. We struck camp about five o'clock a.m., and the ground
being previously made known to the brigades, each brigadier
marched his own brigade. We passed Goojerat on our right.
The citizens were squatted upon the walls and house-tops to
see us pass. I do not know what they thought, but they
looked very strangely at us. The place had a very different
appearance then, to what it had had a very few days before.
The people were then boasting of victory, and flushed with
prospects of success, with Sheer Sing's flag proudly waving

upon the walls, and he telling them that he should drive all the Feringhees out of the country in a few days. As we went along we passed numerous dead bodies, or rather skeletons— the dogs and jackalls and vultures having gnawed and eaten them, even up to the very gates of the city; for the people had buried none, and the bodies lay about as though they were those of beasts! They were cared quite as little about, although they were the fellow-countrymen of the inhabitants. We marched on the same road we came up, driving the enemy before us, on the 21st of the preceding month. Every well we passed was full of dead bodies, and every village deserted and in ruins. All around looked melancholy and desolate. The cropping for miles round was entirely destroyed.

We found one of our missing men: he belonged to Her Majesty's 29th regiment. He was dead, and was in a sitting posture, with his feet in a hollow in the ground, and one foot off. He had received a ball through the thigh, which had broken it. He fell, and was not seen when the line was advancing; so the poor fellow had crawled to this hole, and sat there and died from hunger and pain.

We pitched our camp about 9 o'clock a.m., with our right on the river Chenaub. The whole of the cavalry was on the right, next the river, on account of the water for the cattle. We were upon a beautiful piece of ground, as level as it could be. I saw our chief riding along the camp, and the field-chaplain with him.

Saturday, the 17th of March, being the "seventeenth of Ireland" (as our men called it) or, properly, "St. Patrick's Day," our band went at an early hour and played "Patrick's day in the morning" at the Commander-in-chief's tent, he being an Irishman, and as full of spirits as ever. He ordered a dram of grog per man to the whole of the European troops.

On Sunday morning Sheer Sing came into camp under a strong escort, and Chuttur Sing with him. The vanquished army were coming into our camp by hundreds. Their arms were taken from them, and they were sent across the river to their homes. Their horses were also taken from them. The Commander-in-chief's minister performed divine service on this day, being the first time we had heard it for twelve months.

On Monday, Sheer and Chuttur Sing were sent forward to Lahore, under an escort of 500 men. The disarmed army still continued coming in. Their horses were taken from them by the prize agent, and they were sent across the river to their homes. They had some Arab horses, as beautiful as ever eyes were set upon, and they were as fine-looking men as ever drew swords. We seemed like children by the side of them. They were well-made, and bold-looking, and I wonder how such boys as we were beat them; but it was through having a good heart, steadiness in the field under a heavy fire, and a determined spirit, and the will of the Christian's God. The prisoners were in their full uniform and were easily known. They did not deny being Sheer Sing's soldiers, and it appeared they did not mind who they fought for. They wanted to enlist into our service: they would fight for those who paid them best. Our baggage went across the river in the evening to Wuzeerabad, and we had orders to march in the morning.

On Tuesday, the 20th, we struck our camp at four o'clock, a.m., and marched to the river Chenaub. We crossed it by a bridge of boats, which took us a long time, as the camels with the baggage could only go by one at a time, or in a single string. They were tied one behind another, by a dozen in a length. The cunning elephants would not cross the boats. They swam through the river. It was eleven o'clock before the whole of the baggage was over. The river had large beds of sand on either side. It was here upwards of a mile across. After we had gone over, we came to the city of Wuzeerabad, about two miles on this side; but there was a branch of the river flowing close by the walls.

It is a fine place, but not so very large. The main street, which we marched up, is a very good one: it is wide and regular, and paved with bricks put in squares. The houses are well-built, and the walls painted in beautiful colours, with the shapes of animals and reptiles of various kinds, and trees and flowers, thus having a splendid appearance. We passed through a delightful garden, where the trees were set out in regular rows, and walks were well laid out in different parts; and in the centre I saw a large fountain throwing up the water in five different places. It was in a square area, having a fountain at each corner, with the larger one in the centre. I think I never saw anything so beautiful, and the scent from the flowers was better than all. This was by far the cleanest and best town I ever saw in this country. I took notice, too, that the greater part of the houses were whitewashed, which put me in mind of " Old England."

As for the women, they are lovely creatures: they are the finest women that ever eyes were set upon. Their skin is fair as the lily, with a blush upon the cheek. They have good features, the eyes being large, and black as sloes, the teeth regular, and as white as ivory, the lips thin, and the mouth well formed; while their long, raven hair, hangs down over their shoulders. The body is well formed, without any useless stays to shape the frame. Their steps are light, and the action of walking free, taking place from the hips downwards, and thereby giving them a fine graceful carriage. Their dress is simple, being a snow-white flowing robe, with silver bangles upon their ancles, which jingle as they walk. Their heads are dressed and ornamented with gold and silver. They are completely bewitching to a stranger.

They appeared well pleased with the conquering army: they were free and pleasant, bowing to us and smiling, and giving us a thousand welcomes as we passed along the town. We pitched our camp about nine o'clock, a.m., about two miles from the town.

On the 21st, Captain Smith of the grenadier company left us for England, on two years' leave, and took a colour with him to Yorkshire. It was a very handsome colour—one which was surrendered to us. We heard that it was to go to Colonel F. Markham's father, as a memorial of the brave deeds done by the regiment the colonel had the honour to command.

I revisited the city on this day, and went to the palace, a fine building, painted all over in the inside in very rich colours. Even the floors of some of the rooms were painted with the shapes of trees and flowers of various kinds. There was some reading on the wall, in the native language. The building was five stories high, and had a fountain upon the top; but it was not playing. From the top there is a fine view of the river, and of the country for miles around. I could see the battle ground very plain, and it would have been a good place to have seen the battle from. It would have been a fine sight to have seen the two armies advancing to the attack.

On the morning of the 22nd, three of Sheer Sing's generals came into our camp upon an elephant. They were fine-looking men: one of them stood upwards of six feet six inches, and another of them had had his arm broken by one of our grape shot, being also wounded in the breast. Dr. Scott (of my regiment) attended to him, and set his limb and dressed his wound. They had a splendid howdah upon the elephant: it was thickly plated with silver, and the seats, too, were covered with silver. One of them said that he was at Mooltan, and that he fought against us there on the 12th of September, and that he remembered Colonel Pottoun being killed, and Captain Balfour wounded. He said we fought more like devils than men. He added that he remembered Captain King, and asked where he was. He (the General) was wounded there that day and so left Mooltan, and joined Sheer Sing after he got better.

On the morning of Friday, the 1st brigade set out on the march at four o'clock. Our band played them out of camp,

x

The brigade was composed of Her Majesty's 8th and 10th, and 52nd native infantry, with the heavy and captured guns, *en route* towards Lahore.

We struck our camp at three o'clock on the morning of the 28th, and marched towards Lahore. Our brigade was composed of Her Majesty's 32nd, with the 49th, 51st and 72nd regiments of native infantry, and two troops of horse artillery, and two regiments of native cavalry. We passed a number of villages, and through a well-cultivated country.

The matters occurring on the several days' successive marches, hardly deserve particular mention. We lost our old Quarter-master Sergeant on the 31st. He had been a fine old soldier: he had served twenty-one years in the regiment, and was well respected by officers and men. He left one little girl to lament his loss: his wife had died some short time before.

On Sunday, April 1st, we pitched our camp at eight o'clock in the morning within two miles of the river Ravee, and on the left bank, and about six miles from Lahore. We now buried our Quarter-master Sergeant. The whole of the officers attended his funeral.

The following orders were given out to us in the evening for the next day, as the army was to be broken up, and the Brigadiers to take command of their own regiments, and Generals, their stations.

General Orders from Major General Whish, C. B., on taking leave of his (the 1st) Division of the Army of the Punjaub.

" General Orders, Camp, near Lahore, April 2nd, 1841, from Major General Whish, C. B., to the Mooltan Field Force.

"In reference to the General Orders of yesterday's despatches, the Major General takes leave of the Mooltan field force under the strongest impression of grateful admiration of their conduct, during the period they have been under his

command, in which every action evinced the most gallant
conduct and steady obedience to the requisition of the public
service, from all ranks; whether in the laborious work of the
siege, or, after the successful termination of it, in frequently
making forced marches, with a view of effecting an early junction with the grand army, and in their various encounters with
the enemy, including and finishing with that memorable battle
of the 21st of February, which led to the total defeat and
wreck of the Sikh army. The Major General assures the
troops of every rank, lately the Mooltan field force, that he
parts with them with his most cordial wishes for their future
welfare.

" W. S. WHISH, C. B., Major General."

*From Brigadier F. Markham, commanding the 2nd Brigade,
1st Division, on taking leave of his brigade.*

"Brigade Orders, Camp, near Lahore, 2nd of April, 1849.

"The Brigadier, on taking leave of his (the 2nd) Brigade,
which he has had the honour to command this last eight
months, requests that officers commanding regiments will
themselves receive, and make known to all officers, non-comis-
sioned officers, and private soldiers under them, his most cordial approbation of the manner in which everything has been
conducted during the time they have been under his command.
To all officers, non-commisioned officers, and private soldiers,
he returns his warmest thanks for the prompt obedience to all
orders, and their steady and gallant conduct in all respects,
whether during the siege and in the trenches, or in action at
Mooltan, and from that to the memorable battle of Goojerat,
which ended the war of the campaign of the Punjaub in 1849.

" F. MARKHAM, Brigadier."

The following orders were some time afterwards sent to us
by His Excellency, the Governor General of India :

From His Excellency the Governor General.

"His Excellency the Governor General offers to His Excellency the Commander-in-chief, to the General Officers and all other officers, non-commisioned officers, and soldiers of the army, the assurance of his deep and unfeigned gratitude for the great services they have rendered to their country, for the zeal and gratitude they have displayed, and for the sustained and cheerful exertions they have made.

"In anticipation of the wishes of the honourable the Court of Directors, the Governor General will grant to every officer and soldier who has been employed within the Punjaub this campaign, to the date of the occupation of Peshawur, a medal bearing the word 'Punjaub,' in commemoration of the honourable services they have done.

"The Governor General has also been pleased to direct that every corps which has been so employed, shall bear the same word, 'Punjaub,' on their standards and colours, and appointments.

"LORD DALHOUSIE, Governor General,
East India."

On Monday the 2nd, we struck our camp at three o'clock, and crossed the river at daylight by means of a bridge of boats, which was a good road. This was the river Ravee. At the place we crossed, it was opposite to the fort of Lahore, and it had a fine command of the river. There were a number of gardens of large size, and walled all round, with a number of trees, having a beautiful appearance. At the river we parted with the 72nd regiment of Native Infantry—as gallant and brave a regiment as ever took the field as a native regiment. They went through the whole of the campaign with us, and in the same brigade. We fought side by side, and I never heard our men say that they saw one of that regiment flinch one inch in the field. They are not the smartest-looking regiment that is in the East India Company's Service, but I do believe they are the best.

On the 6th of November, 1848, three of the companies were engaged with two of ours, when surrounded by the enemy. They repeatedly charged, and fought their way out. They stood firm to a man. When they left us we gave them three cheers, and they returned it, throwing up their caps and shouting "Very good, thirty-second;" and they were very sorry to leave us. The General told them that they should be in our brigade if ever we took the field again.

We forded a branch of the river near the fort, which took us up to our middle, and had a strong current. Two of our men were taken off their legs, and so got a good ducking. We pitched our camp on the north-west side of the city, on a good level piece of ground. Sheer Sing and Chuttur Sing were encamped at a distance from this place, with a strong guard over them. A great number of our men went to the town, and the first thing, as usual, with English soldiers, was to learn where they could get plenty of grog. I went to see the city and fort.

Lahore is not so strong a place as Mooltan, by a great deal, in my opinion. The palace is inside the fort, and is a grand place. There are some gardens very tastefully laid out, and by the side of the walks which cross the gardens a number of fountains, but none of them were at work. All things now appeared to be much neglected, and turned into quarters for officers and soldiers.

There are two walls round Lahore, and a ditch. A branch of the river flows by one side of the fort, and it is well supplied with guns. I went into the city, and found it like all other native towns. The streets are narrow and the buildings high; they appear to be well-built. The streets were clean, but this might be owing to the weather having been fine. I noticed a many good shops. A deal of silk appeared to be made, and a vast quantity of gold and silver lace manufactured in the place.

I saw many gold-beaters.   There were large quantities of
bracelets and rings very handsomely wrought.   The bazaars were
full of fruits.   The people were very independent and no-wise
obliging.   They did not like us being their conquerors, as they
never were conquered before.   They are of a sickly white
colour, that is, the citizens.

Our men soon found the 98th canteen, and long before night
might some of them be seen rolling about drunk, and our guard
tent was full of prisoners.   A draft of men joined us here ;
they were left sick at Ferozepore at the time we took the field.
Our General took leave of us : he gave us a long farewell, and
said he hoped he should have the honour to command us again,
if ever we took the field.   The Brigadiers then took command
of their regiments.

On the day after our arrival I went into the Rajah's garden,
and a fine place it was.   It contained large quantities of mul-
berry trees, full of ripe mulberries—very fine ones.   There
were three different kinds.   I ate a great many of them : they
were the first I ever did eat.   The garden had various other
fruits—oranges, lemons, pomegranates, plums, apples and
pears, and all other kinds of eastern fruit.   A large number of
mosques were round about—very fine, handsome buildings.
Some of the tops were gilded all round, having the appearance
of gold.   One of the old priests told me that they should beat us
yet.   He said that we had never fought fair hitherto, and before
long they should drive us out of the country.

Drunkenness began now to occur worse than ever.   One
half of the regiment, or nearly so, was on duty to look after the
other.   One of my company drank off more than a quart of
grog at a draught, and it killed him.   He was one of the
finest-looking men in the regiment.   He left a wife and three
children to lament his untimely end.   It was a most shocking
thing to think upon, that after going through the whole of the
campaign unhurt, and when within a few days' march of joining

his wife and family, after an absence of nearly twelve months, he should have met with such a fate. What would his wife's feelings be? She was a respectable, industrious woman, and he had been a sergeant until reduced for drinking. We buried him in the evening at the Lahore burying-ground. It rained and thundered and lightened dreadfully all the time, so that we were soaked through. He was buried by a minister, and was the first man buried by a minister while we were on the campaign.

Friday, the 6th, being Good Friday, church prayers were read by the Colonel. The young king of Lahore came through our camp in the morning: he is a fine-looking lad. The elephant that he rode upon was clothed in scarlet trappings, and the howdah which he sat on was plated with gold. He had with him Sir Frederick Currey, the political agent resident at Lahore, and a strong guard of cavalry and infantry.

On the 9th we had orders to march in the morning, and a number of men, and two sergeants, were tried by a Court-martial for drunkenness.

On the next day we struck our camp at one o'clock, a.m., and marched on the road towards Jullundur. We were composed of three regiments—Her Majesty's 32nd and 51st, and 49th native infantry. When the roll was called before starting, three men were absent—one a corporal. We passed some fine gardens, though, as it was still dark, we could see little of them. They were walled all round, and the entrances to them were very handsome at one time, but they appeared to be much neglected when I saw them.

Our road was very good, so we marched with ease. We had no jungle to wind our way through, nor sand-banks to cross, nor grips to break our necks in. The ground was not so well cultivated there as in the other part of the country. The corn was ripe and fit for cutting. We were marching eastward, and in sight of the Himalaya mountains. We pitched our camp on

a good level piece of ground, and near to us was the house of a
French general, at one time in the Sikh service, who had had the
command of this district. It was a very fine house—well built,
and had a good garden attached. It was after the European
style, but was going to ruin.

On Thursday, the 12th, we marched by some fine corn
fields, and came in sight of the fort and city of Umritsir. It
was a very striking sight to see : it put me in mind of approaching a town in England, with its long spires rising out of
the town. The fort is on the north side. We pitched our
camp under its walls, upon the *glacis*. It is a good fort, and in
good repair, with a ditch all round it, forty feet wide and thirty
feet deep. There are two walls, and each of them loopholed
for musketry. The port-holes for the guns are arched over,
so that nothing but the muzzle of the gun is seen. At each
angle is a large bastion, commanding the ditch. I went into
the fort. It has a drawbridge which crosses the ditch at the
gate. Inside are two batteries or towers looking over the rest
of the fort, and mounting three guns upon each. The fort is
not very large, but it is neat and compact. It mounts fifty-four
guns, and is garrisoned by the 1st regiment of native infantry.

I visited the city in the evening : it is surrounded by a brick
wall, which appears in good repair. I saw no guns. The
place is noted for its fine temple, where the natives worship.
I saw it, but I did not go over it, as we were to take off our
shoes to walk upon the " sacred " ground. A number of our
men, and some of our officers did, but I thought by doing so, it
would be showing homage to their gods and images, and so I
would not. The temple is square, and is three stories high :
it is built of white marble, and is gilded nearly all over ; it
stands in the centre of a large square tank of water, perhaps
about 200 yards square. The approach is by a long range of
arches, or bridge, which appeared to be built of white marble,
and the top of it is gilded, and it is very thickly hung with

gilded lamps on both sides. A road runs all round the tank, paved with black, brown, and white marble, set in squares, diamonds, and stars. Three flags were flying upon high poles, gilded : everything had the appearance of gold, and was laid out in the most gorgeous style. I was allowed to stand upon the steps in the inside, without taking off my shoes, so that I had a good view of it. The town was large, and very thickly inhabited. I suppose it is noted for its silk-weaving and cashmere shawls. One of our sergeants bought a pair : he gave between sixty and seventy rupees for them. The town is garrisoned by our Sikh allied troops.

On the 13th we struck camp at one o'clock, a.m., leaving two native regiments here for a few days. No road was cut any further, and it was very bad marching.

On Saturday, the 14th, we marched over a large level plain, upwards of ten miles across. We pitched our camp at seven o'clock, upon the banks of the river Beasse. The waters are very clear. The river is divided into three streams, which wind their way down a large bed of sand. The largest is about 200 yards across.

We struck our camp at three o'clock in the afternoon, and sent our tents across the river, to our next encampment, in order that we might not have so much delay in the morning, as it would then be dark. After starting all our camps, we lay upon the ground for the night, and a rough one it was. About ten o'clock the sky began to darken, and turned awfully gloomy. The thunder began to roll, and the lightning in large flashes spread along the ground. The howling of the wind as it came along was truly dismal. The sands blew in clouds, and even large pieces of earth were blown up and driven about the plain like feathers. We sat upon our beds, to prevent them from being carried away by the violence of the storm. At eleven o'clock awful peals of thunder were heard, and down came the rain ; and rain it did—it did not fall in drops, but in sheets.

Y

All our things were dripping wet; the water was swimming under them : and if we had not sat upon them, they would have been flooded into the river !

At three o'clock in the morning we packed up our wet things, 'and prepared to cross the river. We forded the two first streams, which took us up to our arm-pits; but coming up to the third, and finding it unfordable, we had to cross it in boats. The land on this side is low, and is called a *doab*, or country of much water; for, as we marched along, we crossed numerous small streams running through it. It being now daylight, we could see for miles around; but there was nothing except one level piece of wheat nearly ripe. After marching about four miles through nothing but wheat, we came to another branch of the river. This being a large branch, we crossed it in boats, and opposite to a village. We found our tents about a mile from the place; and it was now about seven o'clock. We employed ourselves the rest of the day in drying our bedding, kitts, arms, and accoutrements. About four o'clock, p.m., just as we had done cleaning and drying our things, another storm came; it thundered and lightened worse than the night before. The wind swept the earth up, and the sand-drifted in large clouds, also tearing down some of our tents. Down came the rain, too, and in less than five minutes our tents were wet through. The whole of the men of my tent turned out, and hung on at the ropes, to pre· vent it from being blown down, and to keep our arms and kitts and bedding dry. The thunder made the ground tremble under us, and caused some of us to reel round—the shocks were so terrible. The storm did not last more than twenty minutes, when all was clear and fine.

On the 16th, we crossed two more small streams, by fording them. The country was well cultivated. We passed through a city of considerable size; it had several fine temples. I saw a number of grand tombs, where some rich natives had been

buried. On one of these graves was the figure of a horse, cut
out of marble; it was in a lying position upon the grave.
There were many peafowl in this place; the peacocks
were very fine birds. The natives here are most of them
Hindoos, and they worship the peafowl. I saw a rhinoceros,
which was very tame, and it was a large one, too. A number
of fine gardens lie round the outside of the city.

We pitched our camp a short distance from the city, at
about half-past seven o'clock. Several natives came into our
camp and went through various performances, and put themselves in many postures. They were very active and clever.

Wednesday, the 18th, was our last day's march, and there
was great rejoicing through the whole regiment. We struck
our camp at three o'clock, and as we took it down, the talk
amongst the men was of it being the last time; and they were
wondering when the next time would be that we should want
our tents.

After marching up to our boot tops in sand, we came in
sight of the city of Jullundur at day-break, and a most delightful appearance it had at that distance. It is surrounded
by groups of trees, which we passed through. The inside of
the city is like all other native towns; the streets are narrow
but middling clean, and the houses are of brick, and some of
them are well-built and high. The town is of good size, but
has nothing about it very remarkable. We entered it by gates
and left it by gates, as it is surrounded by a wall. As soon as
we left the town, I think I never saw anything so splendid in
my life as the country all round this side. The gardens are
full of fruit trees, and the large topes of trees which stand
scattered around contain large temples, towering and showing
their tops here and there through the branches. I saw a large
avenue of trees, green and shady. Some native troops were on
duty in the city, which I was informed belonged to a petty
rajah or prince, who was allowed to keep 9000 troops.

Our barracks were about three miles from the town. We unfurled our colours as soon as we left it, and also the three captured colours. The captured colours were placed in the middle, and the Queen's colours on the one side, and the regimental colour on the other. The captured colours were borne by three sergeants, and our own colours by two officers on the flanks of the sergeants. They were placed in the centre of the regiment, between the 4th and 5th companies. They were the gaze of the inhabitants and officers of this station, who had come to meet us. The Brigadier commanding the station, and a number of ladies, came to meet us. The Brigadier's name was Wheeler—a distinguished officer of the Sutlej campaign of 1845 and 1846. Our band and drums commenced playing, and continued all the way to the barracks. When we arrived at the artillery cantonments, nearly all the men of the station, native and European, had come out to meet us. With them also was a draught of recruits for my regiment, who had just come from England, and this was the first time they had seen their regiment. They looked bewildered. I do not know what they thought of us, but we were nearly all patches. Some of our clothes were patched with leather, so that we were not a very cheering sight for them to see. As soon as we approached the barracks, the band struck up "See the conquering hero comes!" and the whole of the lookers-on commenced a hearty good cheer. When we arrived in front of our barracks, we formed line, and our colours were brought to the front. We presented arms, the band playing "God save the Queen."

The campaign was now over; our colours were marched off with the three captured ones, and we were dismissed to our new quarters, which had not a very cheering appearance. They were built of sun-burnt brick, and they were not finished. The station is a large open plain, and when it was clear, we had a good view of the Himalaya mountains, and could see the houses on the sides of the hills. The sight was most beautiful.

The troops in this station before we went, were two native regiments of infantry, and one of regular cavalry, and one of irregular cavalry, with European and native artillery. It was also the depôt of Her Majesty's 61st regiment. The 61st was the first which occupied this station. They were then at Peshawur.

It was a most feeling sight to see the poor women and children weeping for joy at seeing us approach. They had been left here with but little protection during the war, and were in constant danger, as the few men who were left with them were sick and weakly. I felt deeply for several of the women whom the war had left widows, and their children fatherless. One or two poor creatures sat down on the ground and were weeping most bitterly, and fell senseless.

We found that our new clothing had arrived here a few days before, and we had it served out to us. We stood in great need of it, too, and some of our women arrived in the evening. As soon as they knew to what station we were going, they hired conveyances and came by themselves—rather a bold undertaking, to come so many miles with nobody but the native drivers.

CHAPTER XIX.

A FEARFUL STORM.

On the morning of the 22nd all the women belonging to the regiment came from Umballah, and were looking well. It was a happy meeting for some, and for some it was a most bitter one. The men were very kind to them, and assisted them in everything they could; but the poor creatures stood about weeping, not knowing what to do. The children were clinging to their mothers, crying and asking were their fathers were.

On the 1st of May my company had a merry May dance in the evening, to keep up the old game. The Commanding officer gave us liberty for the evening, and allowed us to have three drummers and three fifers; so we enjoyed ourselves very well. A number of our officers were gone up to the mountains, for the hot season. This station appeared to be very bad for the eyes, for many of our men went into hospital with their eyes affected. For several weeks nothing occurred worthy of notice; but in the latter part of June, the rainy season set in with a heavy storm of rain.

On July 22nd we were visited by one of the most fearful storms ever witnessed. It was very remarkable that for the four preceding Sundays we had been visited by storms of sand.

At four o'clock in the afternoon we had observed one approaching for sometime, but took no further notice of it than usual, except that some of our men said that it looked much blacker than ordinary. We prepared for it by covering up our things, to keep off the sand, as our bedding and accoutrements are always buried in it; for although we closed the doors and windows it always worked through the crevices, and filled the barracks so full that we could not see each other for hours, and even for a whole day at a time.

Some were now lying upon their cots reading, and others were standing. As the black dismal cloud of sand came whirling over and over, the advance guard, or "devils" (as we generally called them) came in front, twisting up the sand in a kind of whirlwind. I was lying upon my cot, reading Carbutt's "Advice to the Young," when, all at once, there came a great rush of wind from the southward, and in a moment I saw the roof of the barracks heave up, and a cloud of sand rush in. I sprang off my cot in a moment, and the door being opposite to me, I was out on to the plain in a second. The book which I had in my hand was torn away, leaf by leaf, until all was gone. I had no shoes on my feet, and nothing on me but my thin shirt and trowsers. I had not gone more than ten yards from the barracks before I was taken off my feet, and pitched forward, head over heels; and at every attempt I made to recover myself I was served the same, until I was carried before the wind for a long distance across the plain. It rolled me over and over, until I was covered with cuts and bruises. At length, I caught hold of a shrub, and held fast by it, as I lay flat on the ground. When I looked back, I saw the poor women driven before the storm, and tumbling head and heels along. As fast as they tried to recover themselves they were swept away with the greatest violence, until I saw several who had not a single thread of clothes upon them. All were carried off them. As for the children, I saw some of them up in the air five or six feet high. While I clung to the shrub, I saw men, women, and children, all driven along together, pitching one over another, and one clinging to another; and as one would strive to save himself by catching hold of another, both would then come down together. To make it still worse, the beams of timber, and large spars, were carried along in the air like so many straws, knocking down all that was in their way;

and numbers were hurt by them who could not get out of their way. Bricks and large stones were sent along like feathers, whilst large trees were torn up by the roots, and swept away as though they had been so many twigs. Others were bent to the ground and broken off, and thus left in pieces. Large hail-stones fell—the largest I had ever seen, or any other person there. They cut the skin so much that many of us were soon all over blood, and the rain fell in torrents. I could scarcely get my breath. The screams and cries of the women and children rent the air, and were wild and piercing, as they were carried along with the storm. It lasted about an hour and a half. When it was all over, the men went back to the barracks to see if any one was buried under the ruins; for the barracks, which two hours before were standing, and all inside still and quiet, were now a complete wreck. Of my company we found, under a part of the roof, two men and a girl. The girl was twelve years old. She was killed. The men were still alive, and we took them off to Hospital, where, after a long time, they slowly recovered.

Only a few minutes before the storm came, the girl had been into my room for some water, and some of the men passed the remark what a fine girl she had become. She was very still, and clean, and industrious; in fact we had not her like in the regiment. Her father, mother, and a child, were all so badly hurt that they were all taken to hospital. Some of the other companies suffered worse than we did, and some not so badly. The right wing had not much the matter. Some of the children were still missing, and were found nearly a mile from the barracks: and, being too young to walk, must have been blown there. One child, not more than a year old, was found lying on its back in a pool of water, crying. None of the children had any bones broken, but were covered with bruises. One woman said her child was taken from her arms, and was taken five or six feet high in the air. Hundreds of birds of all kinds and of all sizes lay dead all over the plain. They, too, had been hurled to the ground by the violence of the storm. The total number of persons killed, was two, with twenty severely wounded, and a large number more or less injured. Had the storm happened in the night the damage done would have been terrible.

On the second of August I made application for my discharge; not because I disliked soldiering, but because I disliked the country. I received it on the morning of the fifth of October, after coming off the main guard, and was then struck off the regiment.

[Here the Author gives an account of his leave-taking, and of the march to Ferozepore, where, on the 1st of December he entered the service of Mr. Brown, the surgeon of the 98th regiment, on the recommendation of Lieutenant Mansell. He then describes the incidents attendant on the voyage down the rivers Sutlej and Indus, which are mainly composed of the sporting adventures of the officers and the deaths of comrades who were invalids discharged from service. The scenes on either bank are briefly pictured, amid which wild beasts are often observed, and occasionally crocodiles and alligators, some of which furnish sport for the officers. At intervals, too, some old Indian fort, dismantled or abandoned, arrests the Author's eye. After crossing the Arabian Sea, the vessel conveying the party of which he was a member dropped anchor in the harbour of Bombay, on the 22nd of January, 1850. Here, to the astonishment of all who had purchased their discharges, they were told they could not obtain a passage to England for a less sum than £20; although they had been informed, on leaving their regiments, that the passage would be only £10. While at Bombay, the Author's master purchased two snakes and two serpents, with the intention of taking them to England. On the morning of the 16th of February, they embarked on board the " Aboukir," under the command of Captain Scott, and laden with a general cargo. Two hundred invalids were also on board. Of the passage little need be said. The usual dangers and breezes were encountered, and inconveniences sustained. At ten o'clock on the

Z

morning of April the 10th, the ship dropped anchor opposite the town
of the Cape of Good Hope, and having taken in a good supply of
water and fowls, it weighed anchor on the 12th.   In about ten days
the barren rock of St. Helena was in sight.   The author gives a passing sketch of it, noticing its church and a few houses on the beach,
and the flight of stairs up the side of the rock, leading to the battery,
whence the guns might be discerned bristling from the portholes.
The author's mode of feeding the snakes on the voyage is rather
amusing.   He became "good friends" with the boa constrictors, but
the snakes were less agreeable. He therefore had to deal with them thus
—as soon as the lid was taken off the case they were in, they usually
raised their heads to come out, when he put the besom on them,
grasped them by the neck, and fed them by inserting a tobacco-pipe
in their mouths, and pouring milk down it.   On the 12th of June,
the "Aboukir" was abreast of the Isle of Wight, and on the 15th
the passengers landed at the Custom House, Gravesend.   From this
point to the close of the narrative, the author will be left to speak for
himself.]

A number of vans met us here, to take us to Chatham.   Two
ships were in the harbour, about to convey recruits to India.
I could feel for them ; as they little thought what they would
have to face.   I felt grieved to the heart for one poor woman,
who had come to see her son off.   His sister, too, was there.
They appeared to be very respectable people.   They both
sobbed aloud as though their hearts would break.   Some of
these recruits shouted as they went into the yard ; but I said
to one, "You should shout when you come back, and then
there will not be so many of you."   We arrived at Chatham
about twelve o'clock, and my master put up at the Sun Hotel.

As several ladies and gentlemen wanted to see my master's
boa constrictors, a day or two after he told me to bring them
into a room, and I got two rabbits for them, when one of them
became very outrageous.   He appeared to be frightened at so
many people, or otherwise at the red flowers on the carpet ;
and when he became so furious the ladies screamed and ran

away, which alarmed him worse. He flew at me, but I parried
him off with the lid of the basket, or a thing made round,
which we kept him in. In one spring he made at me, he
caught me by the right thumb; but I tore it from his grasp,
splitting my thumb end, and taking away a piece of the nail.
I got him quiet at last, and put him up. My master sent them
to London, and I was glad to get rid of them.

On Friday, the 21st, I left my master and came up the river
Thames by steamboat to London, and by railway to Leicester,
were I arrived at midnight, by the mail train. On the following morning I expected to see some of my townspeople, as it
was market-day; so I bought a new suit of clothes, and then
met some of them at the "Coach and Horses," Humberstone-
gate, but they did not know me until I had made myself known
to them. At night I went home to Twyford, and, on arriving
there, I went to Mr. Goodman's, the public-house near to my
father's; for I thought it would be better than going in home
at once, and putting them about, as they did not in the least
expect me. I had sent for my father, by an old neighbour, to
meet me at the public house. On my going in I called for
some drink. In the house were two of my old companions;
one was the very next door neighbour, and was of the same
age as myself. We had been at school together, and play-
fellows: but they neither of them knew me. The landlord
who brought me the ale had known me from a child, but did
not appear to have the slightest recollection of me then. He
passed the time of day, and the remarks on the weather, and
so did my two companions. They eyed me all over, and wondered who I was. While I was in talk, my father came in.
He looked round, but did not see any one whom he knew, who
wanted him. He sat down, and I called to him, and said,
"Come, old man, will you have a glass of drink?" He looked
very hard at me, and came. I handed him a glass, when he
wished my good health and drank. The old man had altered

much since I had last seen him: he stooped much, and his hair was quite grey. He set the glass down, and was going away, when I said, "You had better have another." He stood, and I handed him another. He drank it, and thanked me, and was going away, when I said, "Well then, father, so you do not know me." He was quite overcome. He knew me then. The house was now all surprised. My companions also knew me then, and this caused no small stir in the village. The news soon flew. My mother heard it, and came to see; when she came in she looked round, but did not know me, though I was sitting beside my father. After she had looked round, and did not (as she supposed) see me, she appeared very confused, and said, "Some one said my boy had come, but I did not believe it." I handed her a glass of ale, and told her to drink, and not think of such things; and she was going away quite contented, till I called her back, and said, "Do you not see him?" but she did not know me then, until I said, "Mother, *you* ought to know me." The poor old woman then knew me, and would have fallen to the floor, if she had not been caught. She was some time before she overgot it.

So I had once more arrived at my native town. My companions rang a merry peal on the bells for my welcome. The reason they did not know me was, because I was very dark, from the effects of the Indian sun, which gradually wore off as I got used to my native climate.

APPENDICES.

No. I.

The loss of the British on the Campaign of the Punjaub; names of battles; number lost at each battle; and the times when the battles were fought.

NAMES OF BATTLES AND TIME.	KILLED.		WOUNDED.		MISSING.*		TOTAL.		TOTAL OF WHOLE.
	Officers.	Men.	Officers.	Men.	Officers.	Men.	Officers.	Men.	
Ramnuggur, November 22nd, 1848	1	14	9	54	1	11	11	79	90
Sudoolapoor, and passes of the river Chenaub, December 3rd, 1848 ...... }	..	21	4	47		1	4	69	73
Chillianwallah, January 13th, 1849	22	580	67	1584		104	89	2268	2357
Goojerat, February 21st, 1849	5	91	24	682		5	29	778	807
The siege of Mooltan†	13		51				64	1153	1217
The Grand Total of the whole army									7881

* Missing Men and Officers might be put in the number of Killed, for it was always the case.

† I do not know the numbers of men Killed and Wounded, separately, at Mooltan.

The following is a list of Officers of Her Majesty's 32nd regiment, who were killed or wounded on the Campaign of the Punjaub, in 1848 and 1849, and where they received their wounds. But we lost more by sickness and fatigue than by the sword and ball.

Rank.	Name.	Killed or Wounded.	Where Received Wounds.
Lt. Colonel	Pottoun	Killed.	Musket ball through the belly, and many sword cuts.
Qr. Master	Taylor	Killed.	Musket ball through the belly.
Colonel	Markham	Wounded.	Musket ball through the thigh, making the fourth time—being three times wounded in America.
Major	Case	Wounded.	Musket ball through the shoulder.
Captain	Belfor	Wounded.	Sword cuts, left cheek and ear nearly off, five cuts on different parts of the body, left arm and hand severely cut, by which he lost their use, afterwards died from the effects of his wounds.
Captain	King	Wounded.	Twice wounded—musket ball through the shoulder, 12th September; sword cut on the left arm at the storming of the city, on January 2nd, 1849.
Captain	Smith	Wounded.	A severe cut on the head by a brick, when storming the city at the breach."
Captain	Bryan	Wounded.	Musket ball through the loins, or near the small of the back, very severe—a cripple afterwards.
Lieutenant	Mannsell	Wounded.	Severely, across the back of the shoulders, by the explosion of one of the enemy's shells.
Lieutenant	Birdwhistle	Wounded.	Musket ball through the thigh.
Lieutenant	Jeffrey	Wounded.	Sword cut on the left hand.
Ensign	Swinbourne	Wounded.	Musket ball through the hand.
Ensign	Strawbensey	Wounded.	Severely, musket ball through the the hip—a cripple.

No. 2.

(*From the Leicester Journal of Nov. 16, 1849.*)

The letter from which the following homely yet highly interesting detail is taken, was written by Corporal Ryder, of H. M. 32nd Regt. of Foot, now in India, and addressed to his father, who is an old soldier and Waterloo man, residing at Twyford, in this county. This graphic narrative of a gallant non-commissioned officer deserves to be recorded, as exemplifying the honourable, hearty, and even religious spirit of a British soldier on foreign service. He states that they were almost always in hourly expectation of being in close combat with the enemy; but that he puts his trust in God, who has so often mercifully spared his life, while his comrades were falling by hundreds around him. This document also proves the warm attachment of the men to their officers. He was present at and well describes the siege of Mooltan, having been previously engaged in many other severely-contested battles. In a former letter he observed, that if he was fortunate enough to escape with his life, and chanced to lose a limb in action, he might probably get a medal, which he should feel an honest pride, if he returned home, to wear as a fit companion to his father's Waterloo medal. His defence of the brave Lord Gough does infinite credit both to the head and heart of the writer.—

" Jullundur, India, 21st May, and 9th July, 1849.

" The truth of Lord Gough's proceedings is not put in the papers. It appears to me that whoever wrote to England has been pulling him down as much as possible. They do not approve of his commanding the army. The people who wrote in this way have some dislike to him. I see this in the papers in India. They seem to be pecking at him; but the men who act thus are no soldiers, nor were they ever before an enemy, or they would not be trying to hurt our poor old Chief's feelings like this. But I think I know what sort of people they are like—a certain set who sit in the corner of a room at an inn, with a long pipe in their mouth, puffing out a cloud of smoke, and a glass in front of them, talking over the news of the day. They fill up their glasses and say, *We* beat them again; as though they had been through the hardships of a campaign; and I dare say they never saw a shot fired in their lives, except at a hare or a covey of partridges. These are the sort of men that try to pull at Lord Gough. They would not venture to do so before a soldier that has been under his command, for he is the soldier's friend and a good commander; and if he only held up a finger he would get men to volunteer to follow him through the world; but because he met with bad luck once, he is the worst in the world. Any man is liable to misfortune some time or other; and perhaps he did wrong in being so hasty and not reconnoitering the enemy's position, and in fighting so late in the day. It was not his intention to fight - he was only taking up a position near to the enemy, when they opened a heavy cannonade upon him, and ruffled his temper, and, without any plan of battle, he ordered his troops to the attack.

"The enemy was posted in a large jungle, or thick low wood, and was entrenched, so that it was impossible to see them, or know what strength they had; consequently, our troops were cut to pieces, and the cavalry could do no good. They got into confusion, and were followed by the enemy, and were driven at full speed upon our own camp. This gave the enemy a good opportunity to turn our flank, which they soon did, and got one division completely surrounded. H. M. 24th Regt. belonged to it, and suffered dreadfully, and one battery of field-pieces was taken; but two of the guns were recaptured, so that only four guns were left in the hands of the enemy. Our infantry got into the enemy's battery, and spiked nearly all the guns, and brought twelve away with them. The enemy retired with the rest a little farther into the jungle, our men being satisfied to hold the ground they had taken. The poor 24th lost their regimental colours. You see, then, our army did not gain a victory, nor did they lose one; so you must not believe everything you read in the papers, for there is a great deal of party work in them.

"The Avemundee, a large hill that commands the town of Mooltan, the enemy fought very hard for, but were beaten from it by my regiment. This was the day on which we took the suburbs. On the 27th of December, we charged it and were beat back. Our Major (Major Case) took us about four hundred yards to the rear—we formed line again. He then put himself at our head, and said, 'Come, my lads, we must have it—carry it at the point of the bayonet.' We then gave three cheers, and charged; but the enemy gave us enough to do. They fought desperately. Our gallant Major fell here severely wounded, and a great number of men; *but the Avemundee was carried.* We took possession and held up our caps, and gave a hearty good shout. As soon as we gained the top, and just as we had got the enemy in flight, the 60th Rifles came up and took the flying enemy in flank, and helped them on a bit faster.

"I suppose you see what a large amount of gold and silver, as well as diamonds, we took at the fort. I do not know how much there is, but more than ever was taken before at one place. Our prize money will be a good deal.

"You must excuse me for writing such a long rambling letter, but it has been owing to seeing our gallant old Chief getting no credit for his fighting, and such false statements in the papers. Dear mother, I hope you will give my kindest respects to all the gentlemen in Twyford, and all inquiring friends. I am glad to hear Sir——* is well—nothing gives me more pleasure, for he is a kind-hearted gentleman; and may the Almighty God be pleased to give him a long and happy life, and all his family, for he was always, ever since I can remember anything, a poor man's friend; and may the Great Almighty, who witnesses all our doings, reward that gentleman accordingly! Tell my brother to be sure to learn to read and write, and not to be like myself, always against learning. If I had learnt when I was at home, and had given my mind to it, I can plainly see that I could be an officer in this regiment in a few more years. You know what I have learnt has been since I enlisted, so you see it is never too late to learn. I do not mean to stop any longer than I can help. It is not that I dislike soldiering, but I do not like the

* Sir Frederick Fowke, Bart.

country. Our destination is Cabul. If we go, the hardest of our work will be in getting over the pass, where the 44th Regiment was cut up in 1841, and three native regiments of infantry and two of cavalry, with European and native artillery. This pass is through the Persian mountains; and we must go through it to get to Cabul. There is to be a light division formed of the light companies of regiments, for the purpose of scaling the mountains and heights on either sides, whilst the main body goes up the pass. If this be the case my company will be in it; but God forbid there should be any more war in the country whilst I am in it. But dear father, be assured, if it should be my lot to go again, I shall go without the least hesitation. I have given in my name for my discharge; but if my country calls me to face the enemy, I shall not come home, for it would be cowardly, and the man that would be guilty of such an action would not be worthy the name of an English soldier. Ah, dear father, should the martial drum once more call to arms, and I am called to take the field again, where the loud cannon roars, and the roll of musketry and clash of arms, and the groans of the dying and wounded rend the air—all this I shall face for my country, if called to that duty. Rather than stain the honour of the dear old parents that reared me—rather will I fall in this country than turn my back on the enemy: not but that I would rather be in peace, for, I say, God forbid that I should ever see human blood spilt again! I too well know the hardships we have to bear to have any love for it. No, no; never do I want to see the horrors of another battle field. I have a large book filled with the proceedings of our campaign, every day from the time we left Ferozepoor until we came to this station, which I think will be interesting to you if I live to bring it home. If I return this year I shall arrive in England about April. I shall get my discharge in October, if all is peace. I have now £37 of my own, and £10 more to come for prize money. I shall send you a present as soon as possible; and if I go on another campaign I shall make a will, and send you a copy of it, so that if anything happens to me you will get the money.

"JOHN RYDER,
Corporal 32nd Regt."

www.ingramcontent.com/pod-product-compliance
Lightning Source LLC
Chambersburg PA
CBHW030404100426

42812CB00028B/2827/J